THE GULF OF URENOR

RAGADORN

PLAINS

WASTE LANDS

HILLS

MOUNTAINS

DESERTS

CONIFEROUS FOREST

DECIDUOUS FOREST

SCALE

0   25   50   75

RYME

KADAN

THE BONE HILLS

LUJAR   CLOEASIA

KUCHEK

LAKURI ISLANDS

SAMIZ

VAKAR   VAKAR MOUNTAINS

FERUFEZAN

VASSAGONIA   LOHN

SOUTHERN SOMMERLUND
BEING THAT PART WHICH BORDERS UPON
VASSAGONIA

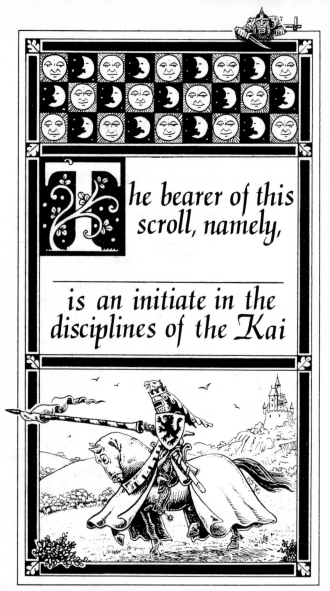

The bearer of this scroll, namely,

_____

is an initiate in the disciplines of the Kai

BOOK 4
The Chasm of Doom

THE AUTHOR AND THE ILLUSTRATOR

JOE DEVER was born in 1956 at Woodford Bridge in Essex. When he first left college, he became a full-time musician with a large London recording studio. Then on a business trip to Los Angeles in 1977, he discovered a role-playing game called 'Dungeons and Dragons' and was instantly hooked. In 1982 he won the Advanced Dungeons and Dragons Championship in America, where he was the only British competitor. He has since appeared on national TV, radio and in the papers in connection with his hobby.

The Lone Wolf adventures are the culmination of many years of developing the world of Magnamund, and Joe looks forward to revealing more of the wonders of the Lastlands in future books.

Born in 1952, GARY CHALK grew up in rural Hertfordshire. Through an interest in history, he began playing wargames at the age of fifteen – a hobby he still enjoys today. When he first graduated from college with a BA in design, Gary spent three years training in a studio before becoming a teacher in art and design.

He was working as a children's book illustrator when he became involved in adventure gaming, an interest which eventually led to the creation of several successful games including 'Cry Havoc', 'Starship Captain' and 'Battlecars' (co-designed with Ian Livingstone). He is perhaps best known for his work on the very successful 'Talisman' game.

Also in Sparrow by Joe Dever and Gary Chalk
Flight from the Dark
Fire on the Water
The Caverns of Kalte

LONE WOLF

BOOK 4

The Chasm of Doom

Written and illustrated by
Joe Dever and Gary Chalk

SPARROW
BOOKS

A Sparrow Book
Published by Arrow Books Limited
17–21 Conway Street, London W1P 6JD

An imprint of the Hutchinson Publishing Group

London Melbourne Sydney Auckland
Johannesburg and agencies throughout the world

First published 1985

© Joe Dever and Gary Chalk 1985
Illustrations © Joe Dever and Gary Chalk 1985

This book is sold subject to the condition that it shall
not, by way of trade or otherwise, be lent, resold,
hired out, or otherwise circulated without the
publisher's prior consent in any form of binding or
cover other than that in which it is published and
without a similar condition including this condition
being imposed on the subsequent purchaser.

Set in Linoterm Souvenir Light
by JH Graphics Ltd, Reading, Berks

Printed and bound in Great Britain
by Anchor Brendon Ltd,
Tiptree, Essex

ISBN 0 09 939180 5

For Bryan Ansell, Rick Priestley and Richard Halliwell

ACTION CHART

KAI DISCIPLINES   NOTES

1	Camouflage
2	Hunting
3	Sixth Sense
4	Weaponskill
5	Mindshield

BONUS KAI DISCIPLINES

6	Tracking

6th Discipline if you've completed one Lone Wolf adventure successfully

7	Animal Kinship

7th Discipline if you've completed two Lone Wolf adventures successfully

8	Mind over Matter

8th Discipline if you've completed 3 Lone Wolf adventures successfully

BACKPACK (max. 8 articles)

1. Crystal Star Pendant
2. 4 Potions of Laumspur +5
3. ROPE
4.
5. Flask of Holy Water
6. Brass Key
7.
8. 1 potion of Alether +2 CS for 1 round Whip

Can be discarded when not in combat.

MEALS

8

— 3 EP if no Meal available when instructed to eat.

BELT POUCH Containing Gold Crowns (50 maximum)

58

EP = ENDURANCE POINTS   CS = COMBAT SKILL

(SEE OVER PAGE FOR SPECIAL ITEMS)

<table>
<tr><td colspan="2">

COMBAT SKILL

3ł

</td><td colspan="2">

ENDURANCE POINTS

30

Can never go above initial score
0 = dead

</td></tr>
</table>

COMBAT RECORD

ENDURANCE POINTS   **ENDURANCE POINTS**

LONE WOLF	COMBAT RATIO	ENEMY
3̶1̶ 2̶9̶ 26	+3	2̶5̶ 2̶0̶
2̶7̶ 2̶3̶ 25	+4	2̶4̶ 1̶8̶ 1̶0̶
3̶2̶ 30	-4	2̶9̶ 1̶9̶ 1̶2̶ 2̶0̶
3̶0̶ 29	+15	2̶3̶ 2̶0̶
LONE WOLF	COMBAT RATIO	ENEMY
LONE WOLF	CO...	

SPECIAL ITEMS
AND WEAPONS LIST

DESCRIPTION	KNOWN EFFECTS
Seal of Hammerdal Summerswerd	doubles points loot on undead
Magic Spear	
Triangular Blue Stone	
Firesphere	
Silver Helmet	
Scroll turn to 84	
The Dagger of Vashna	

WEAPONS (maximum 2 Weapons)

1 Axe

2 Magnus Piers Sword

If holding Weapon and appropriate Weaponskill in combat +2 CS.
If combat entered carrying no Weapon −4 CS.

THE STORY SO FAR . . .

Ruanon is a remote mining province to the south of your homeland, Sommerlund. Nestling between the sullen peaks of the Durncrag and Maaken mountains, the people of this province have long prospered from their toil in the ore-rich mines, living and enjoying their wealth under the protection of their lord – Baron Vanalund.

The gold and gems that are mined at Ruanon yield an important source of revenue to your homeland. The heavily-guarded convoy of wagons that leave the province and journey to the capital has become a regular monthly routine; a routine that had never been broken until one month ago when, suddenly, all contact with Ruanon ceased. A troop of one hundred cavalry from the King's Guard were immediately despatched to investigate the whereabouts of the missing convoy. Their commanding officer, Captain D'Val, was ordered to report back to the King as soon as contact was made, but he and his men have not returned: they too have disappeared without trace.

The King has summoned you, Lone Wolf, last of the Kai Lords, to his citadel at Holmgard. Your quest is to find Captain D'Val and his men, discover what has happened to the missing convoy, and to uncover the veil of mystery that now hangs over Ruanon. The King has gathered a company of border rangers, a unit of élite scouts, all of whom are skilled in horsemanship and outdoor survival. He has ordered these fifty men to accompany you in the hope that, with your leadership, they may succeed where the larger and more visible force failed.

As you and your men enter the Royal Armoury to equip yourselves for the long ride ahead, you glimpse a black crow perched on a window ledge high above. It flies away, but not before a shiver has run down your spine: in Holmgard, the crow is a bird of ill omen.

THE GAME RULES

You keep a record of your adventure on the *Action Chart* that you will find in the front of this book. For further adventuring you can copy out the chart yourself or get it photocopied.

During your training as a Kai Lord you have developed fighting prowess – COMBAT SKILL and physical stamina – ENDURANCE. Before you set off on your adventure you need to measure how effective your training has been. To do this take a pencil and, with your eyes closed, point with the blunt end of it on to the *Random Number Table* on the last page of this book. If you pick 0 it counts as zero.

The first number that you pick from the *Random Number Table* in this way represents your COMBAT SKILL. Add 10 to the number you picked and write the total in the COMBAT SKILL section of your *Action Chart*. (ie, if your pencil fell on the number 4 in the *Random Number Table* you would write in a COMBAT SKILL of 14.) When you fight, your COMBAT SKILL will be pitted against that of your enemy. A high score in this section is therefore very desirable.

The second number that you pick from the *Random Number Table* represents your powers of ENDURANCE. Add 20 to this number and write the total in the ENDURANCE section of your *Action Chart*. (ie, if your pencil fell on the number 6 on the *Random Number Table* you would have 26 ENDURANCE points.)

If you are wounded in combat you will lose ENDURANCE points. If at any time your ENDURANCE points fall to zero, you are dead and the adventure is over. Lost ENDURANCE points can be regained during the course of the adventure, but your number of ENDURANCE points can never rise above the number you started with.

If you have successfully completed any of the previous adventures in the Lone Wolf series, you will already have your Combat Skill, Endurance Points and Kai Disciplines which you can now carry over with you to Book 4. You may also carry over any Weapons and Special Items that you held at the end of your last adventure, and these should be entered on your new Action Chart (you are still limited to two Weapons and eight Backpack Items).

You may choose one bonus Kai Discipline to add to your Action Chart for every Lone Wolf adventure you have successfully completed; then read the section on equipment for Book 4 carefully.

KAI DISCIPLINES

Over the centuries, the Kai monks have mastered the skills of the warrior. These skills are known as the Kai Disciplines, and they are taught to all Kai Lords. You are a Kai initiate which means that you have learnt only *five* of the skills listed below. The choice of which five skills these are, is for you to make. As all of the disciplines will be of use to you at some point on your perilous quest, pick your five with care. The correct use of a discipline at the right time can save your life.

When you have chosen your five disciplines, enter them in the Kai Discipline section of your *Action Chart*.

Camouflage

This discipline enables a Kai Lord to blend in with his surroundings. In the countryside, he can hide undetected among trees and rocks and pass close to an enemy without being seen. In a town or city, it enables him to look and sound like a native of that area, and can help him to find shelter or a safe hiding place.

If you choose this skill, write 'Camouflage' on your *Action Chart*.

Hunting

This skill ensures that a Kai Lord will never starve in the wild. He will always be able to hunt for food for himself except in areas of wasteland and desert. You are aware that the Wildlands south of the Pass of Moytura are a wasteland and that opportunities for successful hunting may not arise until you reach the Ruanon Forest. But this skill is still very useful for it also enables a Kai Lord to move with great speed and dexterity.

If you choose this skill, write 'Hunting' on your *Action Chart*.

Sixth Sense

This skill may warn a Kai Lord of imminent danger. It may also reveal the true purpose of a stranger or strange object encountered in your adventure.

If you choose this skill, write 'Sixth Sense' on your *Action Chart*.

Tracking

This skill enables a Kai Lord to make the correct choice of a path in the wild, to discover the location of a person or object in a town or city and to read the secrets of footprints or tracks.

If you choose this skill, write 'Tracking' on your *Action Chart*.

Healing

This discipline can be used to restore ENDURANCE points lost in combat. If you possess this skill, you may restore 1 ENDURANCE point to your total for every numbered section of the book you pass through in which you are not involved in combat. (This is only to be used after your ENDURANCE has fallen below its original level.) Remember that your ENDURANCE cannot rise above its original level.

If you choose this skill, write 'Healing: + 1 ENDURANCE point for each section without combat' on your *Action Chart*.

Weaponskill

Upon entering the Kai monastery, each initiate was taught to master one type of weapon. If Weaponskill is to be one of your Kai Disciplines, pick a number in the usual way from the *Random Number Table* on the last page of the book, and then find the corresponding weapon from the list below. This is the weapon in which you have skill. When you enter combat carrying this weapon, you add 2 points to your COMBAT SKILL.

0 = DAGGER

1 = SPEAR

2 = MACE

3 = SHORT SWORD

4 = WARHAMMER

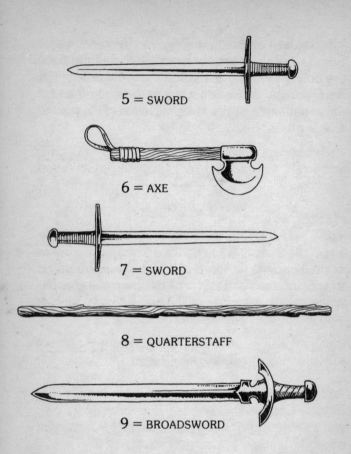

5 = SWORD

6 = AXE

7 = SWORD

8 = QUARTERSTAFF

9 = BROADSWORD

The fact that you are skilled with a weapon does not mean that you set out on this adventure carrying it, but you will have opportunities to acquire weapons in the course of your adventure. You cannot carry more than 2 weapons.

If you choose this skill, write 'Weaponskill in ————— + 2 COMBAT SKILL points if this weapon carried' on your *Action Chart*.

Mindshield

Some of the hostile creatures of Magnamund have the ability to attack you using their Mindforce. The Kai Discipline of Mindshield prevents you from losing any ENDURANCE points when subjected to this form of attack.

If you choose this skill, write 'Mindshield: no points lost when attacked by Mindblast' on your *Action Chart*.

Mindblast

This enables a Kai Lord to attack an enemy using the force of his mind. It can be used at the same time as normal combat weapons and adds two extra points to your COMBAT SKILL. Not all the creatures encountered on this adventure will be harmed by Mindblast. You will be told if a creature is immune.

If you choose this skill, write 'Mindblast: + 2 COMBAT SKILL points' on your *Action Chart*.

Animal Kinship

This skill enables a Kai Lord to communicate with some animals and to be able to guess the intentions of others.

If you choose this skill, write 'Animal Kinship' on your *Action Chart*.

Mind Over Matter

Mastery of this discipline enables a Kai Lord to move small objects with his powers of concentration.

If you choose this skill, write 'Mind Over Matter' on your *Action Chart*.

If you successfully complete the mission as set in Book 4 of Lone Wolf, you may add a further Kai Discipline of your choice to your *Action Chart* in Book 5. This additional skill, together with your other skills and any Special Items that you have found, may then be used in the next adventure in the Lone Wolf series which is called *Shadow on the Sand*.

EQUIPMENT

Before leaving Holmgard on your ride south, you are given a map of the Southlands (see front of this book), a badge of rank that you wear upon the sleeve of your tunic and a pouch of gold. To find out how much gold is in the pouch, pick a number from the *Random Number Table*. Now add 10 to the number you have picked. The total equals the number of Gold Crowns inside the pouch, and you may now enter this number in the 'Gold Crowns' section of your *Action Chart*. (If you have successfully completed previous Lone Wolf adventures, you may add this sum to the total of any Crowns you may already possess. Remember you can only carry a maximum of fifty Crowns.)

You may take your pick of the following items (in addition to those you already possess, but remember you may only carry two weapons). You may take up to six of the following:

WARHAMMER (Weapons)
DAGGER (Weapons)
2 POTIONS OF LAUMSPUR (Backpack Items). Each of these potions restores 4 ENDURANCE points to your

total when swallowed after combat. Each potion contains enough for one dose.

SWORD (Weapons)

SPEAR (Weapons)

5 SPECIAL RATIONS (Meals). Each of these Special Rations counts as one Meal, and each takes up one space in your Backpack.

MACE (Weapons)

CHAINMAIL WAISTCOAT (Special Items). This adds 4 ENDURANCE points to your total.

SHIELD (Special Items) This adds 2 points to your COMBAT SKILL when used in combat.

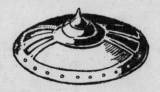

List the six items that you choose on your *Action Chart*, under the heading given in brackets, and make a note of any effect it may have on your ENDURANCE points or COMBAT SKILL.

How to carry equipment

Now that you have your equipment, the following list shows you how it is carried. You don't need to make notes but you can refer back to this list in the course of your adventure.

WARHAMMER – carried in the hand.
DAGGER – carried in the hand.
POTION OF LAUMSPUR – carried in the Backpack.
SWORD – carried in the hand.
SPEAR – carried in the hand.
SPECIAL RATIONS – carried in the Backpack.
MACE – carried in the hand.
CHAINMAIL WAISTCOAT – worn on the body.
SHIELD – slung over shoulder when not in combat otherwise carried in the hand.

How much can you carry?

Weapons
The maximum number of weapons that you may carry is *two*.

Backpack Items
These must be stored in your Backpack. Because space is limited, you may only keep a maximum of eight articles, including Meals, in your Backpack at any one time.

Special Items

Special Items are not carried in the Backpack. When you discover a Special Item, you will be told how to carry it.

Gold Crowns

These are always carried in the Belt Pouch. It will hold a maximum of fifty Crowns.

Food

Food is carried in your Backpack. Each Meal counts as one item.

Any item that may be of use and can be picked up on your adventure and entered on your *Action Chart* is given capital letters in the text. Unless you are told it is a Special Item, carry it in your Backpack.

How to use your equipment

Weapons

Weapons aid you in combat. If you have the Kai Discipline of Weaponskill and the correct weapon, it adds 2 points to your COMBAT SKILL. If you enter a combat with no weapons, deduct 4 points from your COMBAT SKILL and fight with your bare hands. If you find a weapon during the adventure, you may pick it up and use it. (Remember you can only carry two weapons at once.)

Backpack Items

During your travels you will discover various useful items which you may wish to keep. (Remember you can only carry a maximum of eight items in your Backpack at any time.) You may exchange or discard them at any point when you are not involved in combat.

Special Items
Each Special Item has a particular purpose or effect. You may be told this when the item is discovered, or it may be revealed to you as the adventure progresses.

Gold Crowns
The currency of Sommerlund is the Crown, which is a small gold coin. Whenever you kill an enemy and search the body, you may take any Gold Crowns that you find and put them in your Belt Pouch.

Food
You will need to eat regularly during your adventure. If you do not have any food when you are instructed to eat a Meal, you will lose 3 ENDURANCE points. If you have chosen the Kai Discipline of Hunting as one of your skills, you will not need to tick off a Meal when instructed to eat (unless you are in an area of wilderness where the opportunity for hunting is limited).

Potions of Laumspur
These are healing potions that can restore 4 ENDURANCE points to your total when swallowed after combat. There is enough for two doses only. If you discover any other potions during the adventure, you will be informed of their effect. All potions are Backpack Items.

22

RULES FOR COMBAT

There will be occasions during your adventure when you have to fight an enemy. The enemy's COMBAT SKILL and ENDURANCE points are given in the text. Lone Wolf's aim in the combat is to kill the enemy by reducing his ENDURANCE points to zero while losing as few ENDURANCE points as possible himself.

At the start of a combat, enter Lone Wolf's and the enemy's ENDURANCE points in the appropriate boxes on the Combat Record section of your *Action Chart*.

The sequence for combat is as follows:

1. Add any extra points gained through your Kai Disciplines to your current COMBAT SKILL total.

2. Subtract the COMBAT SKILL of your enemy from this total. The result is your *Combat Ratio*. Enter it on the *Action Chart*.

Example

Lone Wolf (COMBAT SKILL 15) is ambushed by a Winged Devil (COMBAT SKILL 20). He is not given the opportunity to evade combat, but must stand and fight as the creature swoops down on him. Lone Wolf has the Kai Discipline of Mindblast to which the Winged Devil is not immune, so he adds 2 points to his COMBAT SKILL giving a total COMBAT SKILL of 17.

He subtracts the Winged Devil's COMBAT SKILL from his own, giving a *Combat Ratio* of −3. (17 − 20 = −3). −3 is noted on the *Action Chart* as the *Combat Ratio*.

3. When you have your *Combat Ratio*, pick a number from the *Random Number Table*.

4. Turn to the *Combat Results Table* on the inside back cover of the book. Along the top of the chart are shown the *Combat Ratio* numbers. Find the number that is the same as your *Combat Ratio* and cross-reference it with the random number that you have picked (the random numbers appear on the side of the chart). You now have the number of ENDURANCE points lost by both Lone Wolf and his enemy in this round of combat. (*E* represents points lost by the enemy; *LW* represents points lost by Lone Wolf.)

Example

The *Combat Ratio* between Lone Wolf and the Winged Devil has been established as −3. If the number taken from the *Random Number Table* is a 6, then the result of the first round of combat is:

Lone Wolf loses 3 ENDURANCE points
Winged Devil loses 6 ENDURANCE points

5. On the *Action Chart*, mark the changes in ENDURANCE points to the participants in the combat.

6. Unless otherwise instructed, or unless you have an option to evade, the next round of combat now starts.

7. Repeat the sequence from Stage 3.

This process of combat continues until the ENDURANCE points of either the enemy or Lone Wolf are reduced to zero, at which point the one with the zero score is declared dead. If Lone Wolf is dead, the adventure is over. If the enemy is dead, Lone Wolf proceeds but with his ENDURANCE points reduced.

A summary of Combat Rules appears on the page after the *Random Number Table*.

Evasion of combat

During your adventure you may be given the chance to evade combat. If you have already engaged in a round of combat and decide to evade, calculate the combat for that round in the usual manner. All points lost by the enemy as a result of that round are ignored, and you make your escape. Only Lone Wolf may lose ENDURANCE points during that round, but then that is the risk of running away! You may only evade if the text of the particular section allows you to do so.

LEVELS OF KAI TRAINING

The following table is a guide to the rank and titles that are bestowed upon Kai Lords at each stage of their training. As you successfully complete each adventure in the LONE WOLF series, you will gain an additional Kai Discipline and gradually progress towards mastery of the ten basic Kai Disciplines.

No. of Kai Disciplines mastered by Kai Lord	Kai Rank or Title
1	Novice
2	Intuite
3	Doan
4	Acolyte
5	Initiate – *You begin the Lone Wolf Adventures with this level of Kai training*
6	Aspirant
7	Guardian
8	Warmarn *or* Journeyman
9	Savant
10	Master

Beyond the ten basic skills of the Kai Master await the secrets of the higher Kai Disciplines or 'Magnakai'. By acquiring the wisdom of the Magnakai, a Kai Lord can progress towards the ultimate achievement and become a Kai Grand Master.

KAI WISDOM

Your mission will be fraught with danger, for you are about to venture into the bleak and hostile Wildlands of the south. Use the map at the front of the book to help you plot your course to Ruanon. Make notes as you progress through the story, for they will be of great help in future adventures.

Many things that you find will aid you during your adventure. Some Special Items will be of use in future LONE WOLF adventures and others may be red herrings of no real use at all, so be selective in what you decide to keep.

There are several routes to Ruanon, but only one will enable you to reach the mining town and find Captain D'Val with the minimum of danger. A wise choice of Kai Disciplines and a great deal of courage should enable any player to complete the mission, no matter how weak his initial COMBAT SKILL and ENDURANCE points score. Successful completion of previous LONE WOLF adventures is not essential for the success of this quest.

Good Luck!

1

For three days you lead your brave company of rangers across the lush plains of southern Sommerlund on the first stage of your urgent mission. The flat treeless fields surround you with a seemingly endless expanse of wheat, so high that even though you are in the saddle it reaches well above your knees. Your horses seem to be swimming through a vast yellow sea of corn that is only interrupted by an occasional track, or group of isolated farmhouses.

The southerners welcome your sudden appearance, but you only make the briefest stops for food and rest neither wishing to risk becoming a burden nor alarm these good people with your mission.

By noon on the fourth day, you reach the pass of Moytura. Here the plains give way to the broken foothills of the Durncrag mountains. You soon reach a highway, the surface cracked and full of potholes, heading off towards the south. This is the notorious Ruanon Pike. South of the pass, the Ruanon Pike crosses a hundred miles of open territory known as 'Raider's Road'. Bandit tribes from the Wildlands and Giak war-bands from the mountains of the west frequently ambush those who travel along the Pike, and the regular shipment of gold and gems from the mines at Ruanon have sometimes yielded rich pickings to these merciless robbers.

'Point and flankers,' you shout, and immediately three groups of rangers peel away from the column and spur their horses to a gallop. You watch with pride as the expert horsemen take up their scouting positions to the front and side of the company.

It is late afternoon when a ranger scout approaches the company from the west. He points towards a craggy outcrop where a thin spiral of wood smoke betrays a hut hidden beneath the overhanging rock.

If you wish to investigate the hut, turn to **160**.
If you wish to ignore the hut and continue on your ride along the Ruanon Pike, turn to **273**.

2

You search the bodies of the dead bandits and discover the following items:

Sword
Mace
Dagger
Warhammer
12 Gold Crowns
Backpack
Enough food for 2 Meals

You may take any of the above items but be sure to mark them on your *Action Chart*.

Picking up the map that lies on the bloodstained table, you notice that the room in which you now stand has been surrounded by a circle of black ink. The map reveals that a door in the far wall opens on to a passageway leading directly to the surface. Eager to leave the death-filled chamber, you pass through the door and run steadily along the passageway towards a distant shaft of sunlight. It takes several seconds for your eyes to adjust to the glare of the sun, but gradually you realize that you have finally escaped from the Maaken mines, and are in the western foothills less than two miles from Ruanon itself.

However, several bandit warriors can be seen patrolling an entrance to the mines, just below the rocky ledge on which you now crouch. If you are to reach Ruanon alive, you must avoid these patrols at all costs.

Waiting until the enemy patrols have disappeared from view, you make your way down a steep track leading into a copse of densely packed trees. A brief pause for breath is all that you allow yourself before setting off through the forest towards Ruanon.

Turn to **200**.

3

You climb the barricade and shout the order: 'Draw bows!' And, as the enemy shield-wall closes fast in a deadly race to beat your archers, 'Fire!'

Their shields of cured skin and wood are no defence against the hail of death that tears into their ranks. The whole line seems to pause and sway; great gaps appear and spearmen fall in heaps on the field. Few escape being injured.

You sense a turn in the tide of battle. The enemy are pulling away from the barricades by the score, carrying their wounded on their backs and on their upturned shields.

You jump from the wall and race back towards the watchtower where Captain D'Val is still embroiled in a bitter struggle against the bandit horsemen. You are about to leap over the body of a dead bandit warrior when he suddenly comes to life and lashes out at your legs with a mace. He was only feigning death and his surprise attack has knocked you to the ground. You lose 1 ENDURANCE point.

Turn to **62**.

4

You recognize the fungi to be Calacena. The spores of these pink mushrooms are much sought after by illusionists and magicians, although it is said that they can cause terrible hallucinations and even madness. As you step gingerly along the corridor, you take great care not to tread or brush against the spore-laden fungi.

The tunnel continues uninterrupted for several miles before eventually reaching a long, deserted gallery.

Turn to **40**.

5

You push him to the ground and smother him with your Kai cloak. The flames are soon extinguished and you draw away your cloak to see how badly he is injured. Your quick action has saved the Captain's life for although his uniform is burnt and tattered, he has survived the fire unscathed.

'It is my turn to thank you, Lone Wolf. This time it is you who has saved me from certain death.'

You help the Captain to his feet and race to the barricade; the enemy have now reached the ruined perimeter of Ruanon, and they are creeping forward under cover of the broken cottage walls. Climbing up on to an overturned wagon, you order the Sommlending guards back to the barricades. But is it too late to repel the attack?

Turn to **186**.

6

You soon reach a junction where the track meets the main highway. Abandoned at the side of the road is a burnt-out wagon.

If you wish to investigate the wagon, turn to **80**.
If you decide to ignore the wagon and ride south along the highway, turn to **175**.

7

Your enemy falls from the saddle and his body is dragged away by his horse, a twisted foot ensnared in the stirrup. All around you the din of battle rages. You realize that these armour-clad horsemen are no ordinary bandit clan; they fight with a discipline and skill unheard of among the lowly outlaws of the Wildlands.

A horse passes close by, the dead body of a ranger still upright in the saddle. You snatch the reins and retrieve a war-horn from the dead man's neck. If you are to avoid total disaster, you know that you must quickly sound the retreat.

You wheel your steed towards the south and spur the blood-spattered animal to the gallop. The remnants of your company are close at your heels, the victory cries of your foe resounding in their ears.

Turn to **154**.

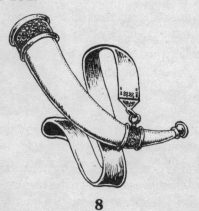

8

Your men secure the boat to a rusty iron ring before following you up the stone steps towards the archway. As you reach a narrow ledge at the top of the granite staircase, you hear strange sounds drifting from the darkness ahead, like the hissing of a jet of steam. It lasts for a few seconds before the crack of a whip and the voice of a man cursing brings it to an abrupt halt.

If you wish to enter the tunnel, turn to **151**.

If you decide not to enter the tunnel, you can return to the rowing boat and continue along the underground river by turning to **240**.

9

A wave of panic knots your stomach as the bridge drops away beneath your feet. You dive forward and just manage to grasp hold of the slatted wooden floor. But the worst is yet to come. Your grip is slipping, and the bridge is about to crash into the far wall.

If you wish to tighten your grip and brace yourself for the shock of impact, turn to **112**.

If you decide to leap clear of the swinging bridge into the unknown depth of the mine shaft, turn to **342**.

10

The warrior staggers back and tumbles over the ramparts into the raging battle below. His feathered mount ascends and flies away, its hideous caw piercing the storm-black sky.

Lying upon the gore-stained floor is a beautiful Onyx Medallion, which was torn from the warrior's armour as he fell. If you wish to keep the Onyx Medallion, place it in your pocket and mark it on your *Action Chart* as a Special Item.

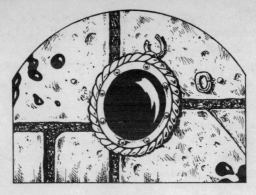

Leave the watchtower by turning to **59**.

11

You have covered less than twenty yards when you reach a solid rockface. It is a dead end. The tunnel has only just been recently excavated and you can go no further in this direction. You must now return to the junction.

Pick a number from the *Random Number Table*.

If the number you have picked is *0–4*, turn to **97**.
If the number is *5–9*, turn to **190**.

12

Fifty miles south of Ruanon, the ruined city of Maaken teeters on the brink of Maakengorge. A cold sweat breaks out upon your brow as you contemplate the difficulty of your mission for you are separated from your goal by fifty miles of enemy-held territory. But there is still a flicker of hope; with the enemy in confusion and retreat, your chances of success will be far higher now than before the battle.

Before you set off on your perilous mission, Captain D'Val offers you the choice of the following equipment and provisions:

Enough food for 3 Meals
Rope
Potion of Laumspur – Restores 4 ENDURANCE
   points when swallowed after combat
Sword
Spear

Make the necessary adjustments to your *Action Chart* before turning to **140**.

13

The show finally comes to an end and you make the necessary preparations for a night's sleep. At dawn the next day, you and your company bid farewell to the travelling players and continue on your way to Ruanon.

Pick a number from the *Random Number Table*.

If the number you have picked is 0–4, turn to **171**.
If the number is 5–9, turn to **25**.

14 – *Illustration I (overleaf)*

Your rangers spread out and move stealthily forward under cover of the large boulders. When you are almost close enough to reach out and touch the enemy, you give a piercing whistle – the signal to attack! In unison, your men rise up and strike. Two bandits die instantly, their skulls cloven in two by ranger swords. A third turns to run, but he is felled from behind and swept away in the foam-flecked water. Your target is a formidable looking warrior;

I. Your target is a formidable bandit warrior

great bracers of steel encase his wrists and a grim necklace of shrunken skulls adorns his leather battle-jerkin. You strike first, but his reactions are lightning fast. He turns your blow aside with his spear and lunges at your face.

Bandit Warrior: COMBAT SKILL 17   ENDURANCE 28

If you wish to evade combat at any time, you can dive into the River Xane by turning to **31**.

If you win the combat, turn to **146**.

15

You have ridden less than a hundred yards when you notice fresh hoof prints in the dust of the winding track.

If you have the Kai Discipline of Tracking, turn to **264**.

If you do not possess this skill, turn to **134**.

16

You reach the door and quickly make your escape. The land behind the tavern is steep and heavily forested. Two of your men follow, but they are both badly wounded and cannot keep up with you. You turn to shout encouragement, only to witness their deaths as they are brutally stabbed to the ground. The bandit murderers wipe their blades and sprint towards you.

If you wish to run straight into the forest, turn to **123**.

If you wish to try to change direction as soon as the trees hide you from your pursuers, turn to **169**.

17

A spear tip has grazed your forearm. It is a mere scratch, yet your arm has become numb and useless. You strike back at your assailant, hoping to catch him as he pulls back, but your blow is weak and poorly aimed. Your vision is becoming a blur; you cannot co-ordinate your movements. Blind terror engulfs you as you suddenly realize that the bandits are using poisoned weapons.

A spear catches you beneath the arm and another sinks into your chest. As darkness engulfs you from all sides, the last sight you remember is the triumphant grimaces of your murderers as they stab you to death.

Your life and your mission end here.

18

You recognize the hoof prints of a Sommlending cavalry horse. There are two sets of tracks and you are sure that they were made by two of your missing scouts. You decide to follow them eastwards in the hope of finding your men.

Turn to **150**.

19

You instantly recognize these amulets. They are the symbols of a Holy Order known as 'The Redeemers', a silent order of pilgrims devoted to a lifetime of prayer and healing. You apologize for your hasty reaction. The holy men both nod their shaven heads in forgiveness.

Your men have pitched camp beneath the marble

canopy, and preparations are soon under way for a good night's sleep. You are hungry and you must now eat a Meal or lose 3 ENDURANCE points.

Turn to **233**.

An arrow hisses overhead; a scream of agony fills the air. The bow slips from the archer's fingers as he sinks to his knees, the arrow lodged deep between his startled eyes. The clack of fangs and the soft swift pad of stealthy feet tell you that the Warhounds are closing in. You look up to see a man running towards you from the barricade. He has a shield in one hand and a longbow in the other; it is Guard Captain D'Val. He reaches you, breathless from his run, and draws an arrow from his quiver. D'Val aims and fires, drawing another arrow from his quiver as soon as the first is loosed. The Warhounds tumble and crash to the ground around you, felled by D'Val's deadly shafts. Eight lie dead before his quiver is empty.

The Captain grabs you by the arm and, swinging you over his shoulder in one swift motion, carries you back towards the barricade. Others run forward to help you, but the bandit archers are now in range and your men are forced back by a hail of arrows. The red shafts of the enemy whistle past on all sides. You reach the barricade and a wagon is pulled aside and you are carried in through the gap. Captain D'Val is close to exhaustion; he staggers and his men rush to catch him before he drops to the ground.

Turn to **341**.

21

After half an hour, one of your men reports sighting a track ahead. The narrow dirt path leads off to the east and the west.

If you wish to follow it east, turn to **134**.

If you wish to follow it west, turn to **191**.

If you have the Kai Discipline of Tracking, turn to **264**.

22

You fumble in your Backpack to remove a Torch, and in doing so, you drop one other Item from your Backpack into the crevasse. (If you were only carrying a Torch, you have lost a Weapon instead.)

You eventually manage to light the new Torch and make your way safely across to the other side of the bridge.

Continue along this tunnel and turn to **157**.

23

You reach the door, but only to find it locked.

If you possess a Brass Key, turn to **282**.

If you do not, turn to **105**.

24

You leap across the warrior's dead body and enter the watchtower. Running up the wide stone stairs, you reach a landing on the first level where two soldiers are firing their bows through narrow oblong slits in the wall. Suddenly one of them cries out in pain and staggers back, an arrow sunk in his chest.

If you have the Kai Discipline of Healing, you can help this wounded soldier by turning to **238**.

If you wish to continue up the stairs to the watchtower roof, turn to **223**.

If you wish to pick up the wounded archer's bow and man his position at the arrow slit, turn to **207**.

25

After journeying through the rich wheat fields of southern Sommerlund, the view that lies before you now looks especially bleak and colourless. The landscape is flat and desolate, only relieved here and there by a ragged copse of stunted firs or mound of broken earth. During the afternoon, storm clouds gather above the peaks of the Durncrag mountains to the west, and the roll of distant thunder warns of imminent rain. It is early evening when your scouts find the ruins of an old temple, less than a mile from the highway.

If you wish to set up camp for the night in the shelter of the ruins, turn to **290**.

If you wish to avoid the temple and continue, turn to **141**.

26 – *Illustration II*

As you run towards the ladder, the dreadful screams of your dying men claw at your ears, as they are eaten alive. You stop and stare back into the tunnel. The Stoneworm is now barely twenty feet away, and is slithering towards you at a terrifying pace. You know that you will never reach the ladder in time to escape. In desperation, you raise your weapon and prepare for combat. The creature is immune to Mindblast.

Stoneworm: COMBAT SKILL 15   ENDURANCE 38

If you win the combat, turn to **321**.

27

You leap over the side of the wagon and sprint towards a line of densely packed trees less than twenty yards from the track. Luck is with you, for the bandit guards fail to notice your daring escape and the wagons continue on their way towards the gantry

Pausing just long enough to catch your breath, you give silent thanks to the stranger who helped you, before pressing onwards through the trees.

Turn to **200**.

28

As the warrior lets out his last dying gasp of pain, he topples back into the mine shaft and plummets into the darkness. His men seem stunned by your fighting prowess, and trip over each other in their haste to escape a similar fate. As the sound of their hurried footsteps disappears along the tunnel, you quickly cross the bridge and leave the chamber through a tunnel in the west wall.

Turn to **348**.

II.   The Stoneworm slithers towards you at a terrifying pace

29

The Torch burns fiercely for just a few seconds before it splutters and dies. You try to relight it but it is hopeless – it simply will not burn. If you possess other Torches in your Backpack, you will also discover that for some mysterious reason, they will no longer light.

If you possess a Firesphere, turn to **168**.

If you wish to continue in the dark, turn to **246**.

If you wish to leave the vault and attempt an entry via the guarded crypt door, turn to **183**.

30

The long night ride and the lack of sleep begins to tell on both your men and their horses. No matter how hard you urge your company on, you cannot out-distance the bandit horde.

Suddenly, a large force of armoured horsemen appear from behind a shallow ridge to your left. They are trying to cut across and block the highway. As your paths converge, you brace yourself for the imminent confrontation.

Turn to **176**.

31

The water is swift, dark and very cold. You tumble helplessly downstream as the irresistible current carries you towards a new and unforeseen danger: white water! The hiss of the rushing water fills your ears. You gulp a lungful of air and brace yourself, for it is now too late to avoid the torrential rapids that lie ahead.

Pick a number from the *Random Number Table*.

If the number you have picked is *0–4*, turn to **272**.
If the number you have picked is *5–9, turn to* **329**.

32

The hideous creature uncoils itself from your legs and sinks into the water. You are elated by your victory, but your lungs feel as if they are on fire. You claw your way upwards until you eventually reach the surface, choking and gasping for air.

The only sign of the rowing boat and your men that remains on the surface of this dark and dreadful river, is a splintered oar floating nearby. You hook your arm over this and drift with the current towards the far bank. A check of your Backpack and pockets reveals that nothing was lost during your struggle in the water, but this discovery comes as cold comfort now your brave company is no more.

Steeling yourself against the unknown dangers that may lie ahead, you resolve to reach Ruanon and uncover the veil of mystery that surrounds it. But first you allow yourself one last look at the black river before you enter the east tunnel.

Turn to **309**.

33

It is almost dark when you reach the edge of a densely forested valley. You can just make out the highway disappearing into the trees ahead, and catch sight of a signpost pointing towards the south. You are now only forty miles from Ruanon, but your men are tired and in need of food and rest.

If you wish to set up camp at the edge of the forest, turn to **74**.

If you wish to send some men into the valley to scout for bandits, turn to **139**.

If you decide to go without food and sleep and press on to Ruanon as quickly as possible, turn to **251**.

34

The creature is flooded by the golden light of your sword. A look of terror crosses its ghoulish face and it hurls itself upwards to avoid your sword blow. You brace yourself for another onslaught but it never comes; your silent attacker has escaped into a fissure in the ceiling.

Sheathing your sword, you prepare to continue. You notice a low portal in the vault wall leading to a long and narrow corridor.

If you wish to continue along the corridor, turn to **235**.

If you wish to leave the vault and attempt to enter the temple via the guarded crypt door, turn to **270**.

35

Using your Kai skill, you blend into the shadows of the chamber wall and slowly inch your way nearer

and nearer to the bridge. Suddenly, the guard puts
down his block of wood and turns his back: he is
rummaging in his haversack for some food. You see
your chance and sprint towards the bridge, your
weapon poised to strike down the unwary guard.

Pick a number from the *Random Number Table*. If
you have the Kai Discipline of Hunting, or if you have
reached the Kai rank of Guardian or higher, then add
3 to the number you have picked.

If your total is now *0–7*, turn to **147**.
If your total is now *8–12*, turn to **231**.

36

The Warhounds lope towards you at an unnerving
speed. You can see their great red-lipped jaws clearly
and hear the clacking of their fangs. You fight to
control your breathing, to concentrate all your
warrior skills, for you must despatch the Warhounds
quickly and with precision if you are to avoid being
torn to pieces. Two dogs, faster than their brothers,
break free of the pack and close upon you. They leap
simultaneously, their slavering jaws spread wide for
attack. You dive forward and roll, striking at their
bellies from beneath as they pass above. Both howl
with rage and pain and tumble lifeless to the ground.

You are back on your feet as the next Warhound
attacks.

Vassagonian Warhound:
COMBAT SKILL 17   ENDURANCE 25

If you win this combat in 3 rounds or less, turn to
155.
If the combat lasts longer than 3 rounds, turn to
277.

You signal to the driver to stop. The wagons halt and a small, moon-faced man in a bright pink tunic throws open the rear door of the leading carriage. He shouts and curses the driver as he descends the ladder, pausing only to adjust the cummerbund that barely covers his huge stomach. Seeing your men, he lets out a strangled shriek and fumbles for a short sword hanging at his side. 'Bandits! Robbers!' he cries, and wrestles to free his sword from its ornate scabbard. A row of anxious faces appears at the wagon windows, but the expressions soon change to a smile when they recognize your Sommlending uniforms.

'Calm yourself, Yesu,' shouts an elderly woman. 'They are Sommlending rangers. They will not steal your gold.' Laughter ripples along the carriages as the little fat man suddenly unsheathes his sword with such force, that he spins around and tumbles to the ground.

'You must forgive Yesu,' says the old woman. 'He means you no harm. "Raider's Road" has made him a nervous wreck.'

You question the old woman, asking her where they have come from and their destination. You learn that they are a troupe of players and have journeyed many miles from their native land of Cloeasia in the east. They last played for the people of Eshnar but it was a disappointing show. It seems that the town was as quiet as the grave; those who did come to see them were a sad and sorry crowd. They are now bound for Holmgard, and hopefully a more appreciative audience.

III.   The little fat man spins around and tumbles to the ground

38

'Light is fading,' remarks the old woman. 'Perhaps you and your men will camp with us tonight? We would deem it an honour, and would be happy to entertain you all with songs and dancing. You notice a hopeful look in the eyes of your men as they await your decision.

If you wish to set up camp with the troubadours, turn to **182**.

If you decide to press on to Ruanon, turn to **247**.

38

No cargo remains inside the charred shell of the wagon. The wood is black and the metal fittings have buckled and blistered in the heat. However, in spite of the damage, you find enough proof from the ashes to confirm your suspicions. This is the wreck of a Sommlending cavalry wagon, one of three that left for Ruanon with Captain D'Val's troop over a month ago.

As you stand in the wagon, brushing the ash from your hands, one of your men suddenly cries out in pain. You glance up in time to see him fall from his horse, a disc of sharp steel embedded in his chest. 'Ambush! Take cover!' you shout, as more of the deadly discs whistle out of the trees to claim their victims. Frightened horses gallop in all directions, your men desperately clinging to the reins. The hidden attackers vanish as quickly as they came, but not before three of your men are left dead upon the highway.

After burying your dead, you must decide on the best course of action; for now only four men remain at your side and the hidden enemy may return at any time to finish their evil handiwork.

If you wish to continue along the highway, riding full speed for Ruanon, turn to **297**.

If you wish to avoid the main highway and continue by the eastern track, turn to **15**.

39

The arrow arcs through the smoke-blackened sky and pierces the officer's shining breastplate. You hear his scream of pain ring out above the din of battle and watch as his cruel eyes flicker and close. He swoons and slips from his saddle, your arrow lodged deep in his heart.

Turn to **148**.

40

A line of empty ore wagons lie parked along a stretch of track that disappears into the west wall of this gallery. Above the arched tunnel, a flight of wooden stairs leads to a smaller passage lit by a spluttering torch.

You stay hidden in the shadows, watching the gallery for half an hour before you are satisfied that it is safe to enter.

If you wish to follow the wagon track into the west tunnel, turn to **55**.

If you wish to climb the stairs to the balcony and explore the passage, turn to **291**.

If you have the Kai Discipline of Tracking *and* if you have reached the Kai rank of Aspirant, turn to **349**.

41

You recognize the silky fluid; it is the trail of a Stone-worm, a dangerous subterranean predator. You warn your men not to step in the slime, for it is highly corrosive. No sooner have the words left your mouth than there is a sudden and ghastly noise.

Turn to **276**.

42

Your knees shatter on impact and you drop like a stone into the darkness of the shaft, but the pain and shock soon fades into unconsciousness. As you hit the surface of an underground river, hundreds of feet below, you are unable to save yourself from death by drowning.

Your mission and your life end here.

43

If you are to survive this attack, you must fight with speed and accuracy. You raise your weapon poising yourself to strike.

Pick a number from the *Random Number Table*. If you possess the Kai Discipline of Mind Over Matter *or* Weaponskill, add 1 to the number you have picked. If you possess the Kai Discipline of Hunting *or* Sixth Sense, add 2 to the number you have picked.

If your total is now *0–6*, turn to **262**.
If it is 7 or more, turn to **111**.

44

As the rangers encircle the ruins, the strangers make a dash for the highway. Your men give chase and swiftly despatch them with their swords. One of the robed men shatters a small flask as he falls to the ground. A search of the bodies reveals 12 Gold Crowns and enough food for two Meals. You notice that both of the men wear amulets on chains around their necks. They are wooden and shaped in the likeness of fish. If you wish to keep any of these Items, remember to mark them on your *Action Chart*.

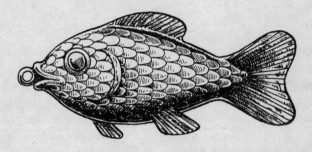

If you have the Kai Discipline of Healing, turn to **149**.

If you do not possess this skill, turn to **188**.

45

You recognize Gnadurn sap dripping from their spears. It is a deadly poison. You dare not risk engaging in combat with these bandits, for the merest graze from one of their tainted weapons could be fatal. Leaping to your feet, you race away from the trees and run towards Ruanon.

Turn to **307**.

46

You have barely taken a dozen steps when you are confronted by a hideous sight. The tunnel ahead is blocked by a huge and slimy creature, its skin covered with warts that glow with a greenish luminescence. You draw your weapon as it moves closer, hopping from one clawed foot to the other. Suddenly, a pair of wings sprouts from its back and it leaps into the air. You feel your stomach contract as it hurtles towards you, its razor-fanged mouth opening wider and wider.

Tunnel Fiend: COMBAT SKILL 20   ENDURANCE 10

If you win this combat, turn to **281**.

47

You manage to gasp a lungful of air before the dark waters close over your upturned face. A tentacle brushes your foot and you lash out just in time to prevent it from ensnaring you. The creature is badly wounded; but it is determined to claim your life in return for its injury.

Giant Meresquid: COMBAT SKILL 16   ENDURANCE 37

If the combat lasts longer than five rounds, turn to **340**.

If you win the combat in five rounds or less, turn to **32**.

48

You sense that the left tunnel leads away from Ruanon. Without hesitation, you turn and head off towards the right.

Turn to **145**.

49

Lifting your feet high, you step into the tall crops, taking care to part them first with your hands. You allow the stalks to close again behind your back before you crouch down and hold your breath. You have completely vanished from sight; it is as if the stalks have never been disturbed.

The bandits amble past barely inches from where you hide, oblivious to your presence. When you are sure they have gone, you emerge from the crops and hurry away.

Turn to **204**.

50

The great doors open to reveal a patrol of six tunnel guards. They are each armed with a crossbow and react instantly to your presence on the bridge. 'Charge!' you shout, hoping that you might be able to overpower the guards before they can fire their deadly weapons.

Pick a number from the *Random Number Table*.

If the number you have picked is 0–6, turn to **184**.
If the number is 7–9, turn to **267**.

51

You have been riding for over four hours when you see a flock of birds. They are black and very large, and are swooping around the brow of a distant ridge.

If you wish to investigate the ridge, turn to **328**.
If you would rather ignore the birds and press on, turn to **120**.
If you have the Kai Discipline of Animal Kinship, turn to **227**.

52

A hail of feathered shafts cuts the air. The arrows strike home with deadly accuracy. Three of your men have fallen by the time you reach the mine, and an arrow passes so close to your right eye that you are blinded by its flights. You lose 1 ENDURANCE point. With a hand held to your injured eye, you stagger into the entrance of the tunnel.

Turn to **248**.

53

The door slams shut and you spin round to see a bandit leaping at you from the shadows. His head is a mass of bloodied bandages, but he is armed and determined to fight.

Wounded Bandit: COMBAT SKILL 13   ENDURANCE 16

He fights you with his back to the door and you cannot evade him.

If you win the combat, turn to **109**.

54

As you gradually descend into the tunnel, you feel a draught of cold, dank air on your face. The walls of the tunnel are composed of a glittering ore that catches the light of your torch and reflects it in a dazzling display of colour. As your eyes follow the dancing lights you suddenly notice that the floor is covered with pink fungi.

If you have the Kai Discipline of Healing *and* you have reached the Kai rank of Warmarn, turn to **4**.

If you do not have this skill, or if you have yet to reach the rank of Kai Warmarn, you can risk walking through the fungi; turn to **65**.

Alternatively, if you wish, you may eat some of the fungi by turning to **201**.

55

As you make your way along the torchlit tunnel, you pass several ore wagons bearing the same design branded upon their wooden sides: a cross moline above the initials 'O.V.'. You recognize the seal of Oren Vanalund, the Baron of Ruanon, and it confirms the fact that you are heading in the right direction. Suddenly, the sound of approaching footsteps begin to echo along the tunnel ahead. They become louder, accompanied now by shouting and the crack of a whip.

If you wish to dive into one of the empty ore wagons, turn to **161**.

If you wish to hide in the shadows of the rough tunnel wall, turn to **286**.

56

You hit the guard and open a deep wound in his neck. He screams and turns to face you, a short sword in his hand.

Wounded Guard: COMBAT SKILL 12   ENDURANCE 18

If you win and the fight lasts for 3 rounds of combat or less, turn to **69**.

If you win but the fight lasts longer than 3 rounds, turn to **203**.

57

'You must save her, Lone Wolf. You must prevent the sacrifice!' The Baron's voice is choked with emotion.

'Save who? Who must he save?' questions Captain D'Val, as he tries to calm the excited Baron.

'My daughter, Madelon, of course,' the Baron answers. Tears are welling up in his red-rimmed eyes and nervously he wrings his hands. Then he utters the ominous prophecy:

When the full moon shines o'er the temple deep,
A sacrifice will stir from sleep
The legions of a long forgotten lord.
When a fair royal maid on the altar dies,
The dead of Maakengorge shall rise
To claim their long-awaited reward.

'Don't you see? Barraka has found the dagger of Vashna. He is going to sacrifice my daughter upon the altar of Maaken to release the undead of Maakengorge, the chasm of doom.

'During the Age of the Black Moon, King Ulnar of

Sommerlund killed the mightiest of all the Darklords, Vashna, with the Sommerswerd – the sword of the sun. Vashna's body and the bodies of all his troops were hurled into the bottomless abyss of Maakengorge. He plans to lead the dead to victory; first to conquer Sommerlund and then all of the Lastlands,' explains the Baron, fear in his eyes.

You stare at the Baron in stunned silence. If Barraka completes the sacrifice, all is lost. What mortal army can stand against a legion of the dead?

Captain D'Val ushers you from the chamber and closes the door. 'I feared he was insane, and I refused to listen to his words. But the events of the last few days confirm my worst nightmare. He speaks the truth!'

As the dreadful significance of the prophetic verse begins to chill your spine, your thoughts are broken by the shrill blast of a war-horn. Captain D'Val strides over to an arrow slit in the wall and looks out across the desoltate plain. As he turns to speak, his face is ashen grey. 'The bandits – they're launching an attack!'

If you possess Captain D'Val's Sword, turn to **327**.
If you do not possess this weapon, turn to **289**.

58

Peering about in the gloom of the camp perimeter, you decide that the actor can only be in one of two places: a large caravan to your left or a smaller coach to your right. You notice a handkerchief lying at the door of the smaller coach.

If you wish to enter the large caravan, turn to **222**.

If you decide to investigate the smaller coach, turn to **110**.

59

Captain D'Val and his men are locked in mortal combat with the invading cavalry; they are out-numbered and hard pressed by the merciless foe who use their spike-shod horses to kick and trample their opponents underfoot. You reach the barricade to see yet another wave of the enemy approaching. Armoured handlers with packs of Warhounds spread out in front of a line of spear-armed infantry.

Fifty yards from the barricade, the armoured handlers stop and kneel to let loose their dogs of war.

Pick a number from the *Random Number Table*.

If the number you have picked is *0–4*, turn to **193**.
If it is *5–9*, turn to **260**.

60

Your Kai sense reveals that the right tunnel is a dead end. Anxious not to get trapped by your pursuers, you turn and run into the left tunnel.

Turn to **199**.

61

Your lightning reactions have saved you from the river. You side-step in time to avoid the sinuous tentacle and lash out. The blow opens a wide gash and an arc of green blood sprays across the battered rowing boat. Only two of your men remain. One stabs at the tentacle around his foot and the other lies unconscious at your feet, his arm badly broken at the elbow.

> If you wish to hack at the tentacle that is coiled around the ranger's foot, turn to **304**.
> If you wish to aid the unconscious ranger lying at your feet, turn to **136**.
> If you wish to grab the oars and row for the bank, turn to **189**.

62

The bandit springs to his feet and attacks you with his mace. Deduct 2 from your COMBAT SKILL for the first 3 rounds of combat, as you are now lying on the ground. You cannot evade the combat and must fight the bandit to the death.

Bandit Warrior: COMBAT SKILL 17   ENDURANCE 24

> If you win, turn to **148**.

63

The sound of a tolling bell drifts across the barren landscape. Window shutters slam down but eyes still peer at you from the arrow slits carved into the walls.

You draw your company to a halt outside the wide tavern doors. 'We are Sommlending. We seek shelter for the night and fodder for our mounts,' you shout. There is a long pause before a voice answers your call.

Pick a number from the *Random Number Table* to discover the nature of the reply.

> If the number you have picked is 0–4, turn to **259**.
> If the number is 5–9, turn to **95**.

64

The only exit from the chamber, other than the well and the tunnel by which you entered, is by a spiral staircase set into the north wall.

If you wish to ascend the stairs, turn to **170**.
If you wish to descend the stairs, turn to **228**.

65

As you tread on the fungi, the pink flesh splits releasing clouds of spores into the tunnel. They fill your eyes and nostrils. You cannot breathe. Blindly you stagger forward until you are clear of the fungi, but as you emerge from the cloud of spores, you are confronted by another peril. A host of hideous, bat-winged reptiles are flying towards you, their scaly hands grasping jagged pieces of stalagmite. You cannot evade combat and must fight them all as one enemy.

Tunnel Fiends: COMBAT SKILL 20   ENDURANCE 10

If you win the combat, turn to **298**.

66

You land and roll forwards. The Vassagonian leaps after you, hoping to deliver a killing blow before you can rise, but he does not realize he is fighting a Kai Lord. You strike him in mid-air and he is dead before he hits the ground.

D'Val runs past to your left. He leads a dozen of his best swordsmen in a counter-charge, driving the enemy back to the barricade. None escape alive. Those who survive D'Val's swordsmen are cut down by his archers as they run across the plain. But the shout of victory has barely died away when you are faced by another formidable attack.

Turn to **124**.

67 – *Illustration IV (overleaf)*

Your men are hungry and exhausted, but they possess an unshakeable faith in the infallibility of your Kai sense. You give the signal to leave, but as you near the town entrance, you hear a thin whistling noise. A ranger at your side suddenly screams in agony, a flat circle of razor sharp steel embedded in his chest. More of the discs follow whistling down from the rooftops to claim their victims. One grazes the back of your hand before embedding itself in the neck of your startled horse. You are thrown to the ground and lose 1 ENDURANCE point.

Staggering to your feet, you run, half-crouched, to the shelter of a wagon. Two of your men lie dead upon the road, but the others have escaped the ambush and are galloping away from the town, hidden by the rising clouds of dust.

You turn to see a bandit warrior standing at a nearby balcony. He is dark-skinned, with oily black hair and beard. He flicks his hand and a deadly disc whistles towards your face.

If you possess the Sommerswerd, turn to **292**.

If you do not possess this Special Item, pick a number from the *Random Number Table*. If you have either the Kai Discipline of Hunting or Mind Over Matter, add 2 to the number that you have picked.

(contd over)

IV. Razor-sharp discs of steel whistle down to claim their victims

If your total is now *0–4*, turn to **242**.
If it is *5–8*, turn to **263**.
If it is *9–11*, turn to **278**.

68

One sharp blow with the edge of your hand is all that is needed to smash the lock on the boathouse door. Your curiosity is soon rewarded by the sight of an upturned rowing boat resting upon a pair of wooden trestles. A pail of pitch stands beneath it. From the layer of dust covering the surface of the boat, you judge that it has stood undisturbed for several months.

If you wish to launch the rowing boat, turn to **180**.
If you wish to search the boathouse for other useful items, turn to **213**.

69

As you step over the dead guard, you follow the line of the hanging rope to a pair of locking pins, which secures the bridge to the edge of the mine shaft. If the guard had pulled the rope, the bridge would have fallen away and you would have been trapped on this side of the chamber.

You quickly run across the bridge just as your pursuers enter. A rope, similar to the one opposite, hangs from the ceiling next to the tunnel entrance in the west wall. You look back to see that your pursuers are now halfway across the bridge.

If you wish to pull the rope, turn to **125**.
If you wish to ignore the rope and escape into the tunnel, turn to **348**.

70

Your passage through the trees is lit by the flickering glow of the campfires that line the highway. Bandit warriors huddle round drawing warmth and comfort from the flames. They take little interest in their guard duties and you find it easy to avoid their patrols.

By morning, you have reached the edge of the forest. You stare out across the fields of tall crops towards a small village that lies at the base of a shallow valley. The fields are only separated by narrow tracks and these are alive with flying insects, hovering in swarms. You are walking along one of these tracks when suddenly you spot bandits ahead. They are wandering idly up the track towards you, their spears slung over their shoulders.

If you possess an Onyx Medallion, turn to **305**.

If you wish to dive into the tall crops and hide, turn to **159**.

If you have the Kai Discipline of Camouflage *and* have reached the Kai Rank of Guardian or higher, turn to **49**.

71

As the warrior falls dead at your feet, you turn to rally your men. To your horror, you see three of them lying spreadeagled on the stairs, killed by crossbow bolts. The other man is wounded and surrounded by the enemy. As more guards flood into the chamber, he shouts in desperation, 'Flee, my Lord. Escape while you still can.'

No sooner have his words echoed through the hall than a sword blade pierces his heart. You turn and run towards a distant door where a tunnel disappears towards the north. Slamming the door you draw its bolt. As you race along the dusty tunnel you pray that the door will hold and keep your pursuers at bay.

Turn to **348**.

72

The flat Wildlands offer no cover in which to hide from the bandit horde. You know that if you are to avoid combat with an enemy, which vastly out-numbers you, you must split up your company and try to outrun them.

You detach a troop of ten rangers to follow you, and send the remainder off towards the west, in the hope that they may lure the bandits away to the Durncrag mountains.

With one last glance at the enemy, you lead your ten rangers on a deadly race along the Ruanon Pike.

Turn to **211**.

73

You circle the temple, keeping just out of reach of the blue-flamed dagger. Barraka unsheathes a scimitar with his free hand, cutting the air about your head with its mirror-like steel but drawing no blood.

If you possess a Flask of Holy Water, turn to **283**.
If you do not possess this Item, turn to **325**.

74

The night passes without incident and you awake refreshed by your sleep: restore 1 ENDURANCE point. After breaking camp, you enter the forested valley. Your warrior instincts warn you that the highway would be the ideal place for an ambush; the densely packed trees lining the roadside could easily conceal an attacker. As a precaution against such a surprise attack, you send three of your men on ahead with orders to report back if they should sight anything at all unusual.

After travelling some distance, you come across the wreck of a burnt out wagon abandoned at the side of the road. Behind it, a track disappears eastwards up into the hills. There is no sign of your scouts, who should have returned to report this abandoned wreck.

If you wish to search the wrecked wagon, turn to **38**.
If you wish to ignore the wagon and continue along the highway, turn to **175**.
If you wish to investigate the track leading into the hills, turn to **293**.

75

No sooner has the first warrior collapsed when another is hacking at you from the side. As you turn to face him, a spear thrust gashes your left arm and you lose 2 ENDURANCE points. You recoil in pain and, in the crush of battle, you slip and fall to the floor, which is already strewn with bodies. Then you glimpse an open door and crawl towards it.

Pick a number from the *Random Number Table*. If you possess the Kai Discipline of Camouflage, add 3 to the number you have picked.

If your total is now *0–5*, turn to **192**.
If your total is now *6–12*, turn to **16**.

76

The guards will not answer your questions. They seem to be more afraid of what their leader will do if they betray him, than any torture they may face at your hands. All that you can determine from their uniforms and their manner is that they are part of the bandit horde that attacked you earlier.

If you wish to search them, turn to **268**.
If you wish to leave the chamber, turn to **64**.

77

An evil sneer spreads across his savage face. His words sound in your mind although his lips never part. This warrior is skilled in mind combat. Unless you have the Kai Discipline of Mindshield you will lose 1 ENDURANCE point for every round of combat you fight with him. He is immune to Mindblast.

Vassagonian Captain:
COMBAT SKILL 22   ENDURANCE 28

You may evade combat after 2 rounds by turning
to **98**.
If you win, turn to **10**.

78

As you approach they slip back their hoods to reveal
two smiling faces. They seem relieved to have made
friendly contact in the middle of this inhospitable
wasteland. Neither of them speaks, but they remove
amulets from around their necks and offer them as
some kind of identification. The small wooden fish
hanging on the neckchains are symbols of a Holy
Order known as 'The Redeemers', a silent order of
pilgrims devoted to a lifetime of prayer and the study
of the healing arts.

One of the pilgrims hands you a small earthenware
Flask that contains a potion of Holy Water. If you wish
to keep this Flask, mark it on your *Action Chart* as a
Backpack Item.

Your men pitch camp beneath the marble canopy
and preparations are made to get some sleep. You
are hungry and must now eat a Meal or lose
3 ENDURANCE points.

Turn to **233**.

79

Struggling to your feet, you stagger along the forest
track as it ascends into the darkening foothills of the
Maaken range. The track comes to an abrupt halt at
the entrance of a mine tunnel, partially obscured by

foliage. You realize this must be a disused route into the Maaken mines, for they honeycomb the foothills and mountains of this region. You know that if you can locate one of the major shafts, you should be able to trace your way through the mines to Ruanon itself.

Just inside the tunnel entrance, you find a broken crate containing five Torches and a Tinderbox. The tunnel is pitch black and you will need at least one torch to light your way. You may take however many Torches you wish before continuing, but each Torch takes up one space in your Backpack.

The tunnel is cold and forbidding. You explore for over a mile before arriving at a junction. Here, another tunnel branches off towards the south. It appears to be a recent excavation and you follow it in the hope of finding a major shaft.

Turn to **117**.

80

Although the fire has totally destroyed any markings there may have been, there still remains enough of the charred shell for you to recognize its military origin. It is a Sommlending cavalry wagon, one of

three that accompanied Captain D'Val and his troop. It was loaded with food and equipment when it left Holmgard one month ago, but all that remains of its cargo now are heaps of ash. Once you have satisfied yourself that nothing has been overlooked that may give a clue to Captain D'Val's fate, you remount your horse and lead your men southwards along the highway.

Turn to **175**.

81

The hoarse cries of the guard echo along the tunnel. You soon reach a section where repairs are in progress; a prop in the centre of the passage supports a cracked roof beam. If you could just knock away the prop, it might cause the roof to fall in, which would seal off the passage behind you. You can now hear the running footsteps of more than one guard approaching.

If you wish to knock away the roof prop, turn to **173**.

If you decide to ignore the prop and press on along the tunnel, turn to **224**.

82

You have ridden less than a mile when you discover a burnt-out wagon abandoned at the side of the road. Behind it, a hill track disappears eastwards.

If you wish to investigate the wagon, turn to **337**.

If you decide to ignore the wagon and continue, turn to **297**.

If you wish to explore the hill track, turn to **15**.

83

The stairs lead down to a lower level of the mines where a passage continues southwards. You have just entered the passage when a patrol of guards suddenly emerges from a concealed door ahead. You barge through them before they can draw their weapons, but their screams of anger echo in your ears as you sprint towards a faint light in the distance.

Turn to **199**.

84 – *Illustration V (overleaf)*

In the dim light of the interior you see an old man seated at a table. The flicker of a log fire is all that illuminates this foul-smelling hovel, yet it sheds enough light for you to see the clutter of charts and strange instruments that crowd the hut. The man slowly raises his gaze from a large crystal sphere and bids you sit opposite him.

'You know my name – how?' you ask warily.

'The stars foretold our meeting long ago, Lone Wolf,' he replies, slowly passing his withered old hands around the sphere. 'Be not alarmed by my knowledge for I wish only to aid you.' He produces a small scroll of parchment from within his robe and he hands it to you. Upon the scroll is written the following verse:

When the full moon shines o'er the temple deep,
A sacrifice will stir from sleep
The legions of a long forgotten lord.
When a fair royal maid on the altar dies,
The dead of Maakengorge shall rise
To claim their long-awaited reward.

You ask the meaning of the strange verse, but the old man does not answer you. He seems to have fallen into a deep trance. You lean across the cluttered table to awaken him, and are shocked to see your hand pass straight through his body. Gradually his image begins to fade. Within seconds he has disappeared completely.

You place the Scroll in your pocket. (Mark this as a Special Item on your *Action Chart.*) You quickly leave the hut, pausing only to wipe the cold sweat from your brow.

Turn to **273**.

85

You try to draw your weapon but the creature is a swift and deadly killer. Its hollow fangs penetrate your spine, drawing out your life's blood and paralysing your body. You hear the clatter of your weapon as it drops to the floor, but you do not feel pain as you topple forwards, smashing your face against the hard unyielding stone.

Your life and your mission end here.

86

As you leap on to an overturned wagon, you catch sight of two soldiers smothering Captain D'Val with their jackets. You pray he will survive the flames and that you have acted in time to rally his scattered force. The enemy has reached the ruined perimeter of Ruanon, and are now creeping forward under cover of the broken cottage walls. You shout orders to D'Val's men to hurry back to the barricade, but the

V.   'The stars foretold our meeting long ago, Lone Wolf'

enemy are only a hundred yards from the wall; is it too late to repel the attack?

Turn to **186**.

87

The guard is soon joined by more of his friends who give chase; you can hear their quickening pace and their harsh panting breath close behind you. Suddenly the tunnel narrows and divides in two.

If you wish to enter the left tunnel, turn to **199**.
If you wish to enter the right tunnel, turn to **208**.
If you have the Kai Discipline of Sixth Sense or Tracking, turn to **60**.

88

A foul odour assails your nostrils, making you choke and retch. Covering your mouth and nose you step back and raise your weapon in readiness to strike, for the creature is slithering towards you at a frightening pace. Your men rain blows upon its gaping jaws, but their blades barely scratch the creature's glistening grey skin before they are snatched and swallowed whole. Relentlessly the Stoneworm advances until it is upon you. You cannot evade it and you must fight the creature to the death. It is immune to Mindblast.

Stoneworm: COMBAT SKILL 15   ENDURANCE 38

If you win the combat, turn to **321**.

89

Wildly you fight your way through a circle of bandits, guiding your horse with just the pressure of your knees. Ahead you see a ridge of muddy ground and you charge towards it in the hope that you can rally your men. You are approaching the brow of the ridge when an armour-clad warrior charges at you from the side, his spear levelled at your throat. You cannot evade combat and must fight him to the death.

Bandit Warrior: COMBAT SKILL 17   ENDURANCE 26

If you win, turn to **7**.

90

You are in combat with a Vassagonian horseman who is now on foot. You cannot evade him and must fight him to the death.

Bandit Horseman: COMBAT SKILL 17   ENDURANCE 24

If you win, turn to **249**.

91

It is impossible to enter the mine on horseback and you are forced to leave your horses outside. The mine is very dark but you are quick to notice that unlit Torches hang from the walls at regular intervals. You each take a Torch and light them before continuing. In the dim glow you discover footprints leading to a collapsed section of the tunnel. They continue all the way to the top of a huge mound of earth, which reaches almost to the ceiling, leaving only a small gap.

If you wish to climb the mound and squeeze through the gap, turn to **254**.

If you decide to call off the search, you can return to the surface, remount your horses and descend the hill track by turning to **191**.

92

It is noon on the following day when you reach the outskirts of Eshnar. To the south, the wooded hills gradually ascend towards the magnificent snow-capped peaks of the Maaken range. It is a beautiful sight, one of stark contrast to the squalor of Eshnar and the desolate Wildlands to the north. You ride along the only street in this dilapidated town, and eventually arrive outside a large tavern called 'The Pick and Shovel'. Your men are exhausted and badly in need of food and rest.

If you wish to enter the tavern, turn to **132**.

If you decide to continue along the street, turn to **301**.

If you have the Kai Discipline of Sixth Sense, turn to **210**.

93

Four swarthy-faced bandits are seated at a round table, a plan of the mines spread before them. Surprise barely has time to register upon their faces before you launch your deadly attack; three are despatched even before they have drawn their weapons. The fourth rolls away from his dead

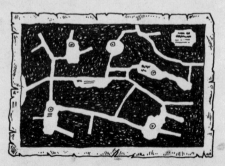

companions and unsheathes his sword. The fire of revenge burns bitterly in his eyes as he lunges towards you.

Bandit Warrior: COMBAT SKILL 15   ENDURANCE 26

If you win the combat, turn to **2**.

94

Suddenly, the boat lurches forward and you are catapulted into space. You tumble for what seems like an eternity before hitting deep water with such breathtaking force that you plunge down over twenty feet. The icy water stuns you and saps your strength. You are desperate for air. You fight to reach the surface but your Backpack drags you down; you must discard it or you will certainly drown.

When you reach the surface, you are caught by the swift current and swept away from the waterfall. You are soon washed up upon a gravel bank at the bottom of a steep ravine.

You have lost your Backpack and everything it contained, as well as your boat and your men. But in spite of this calamity, you are still alive and relatively unharmed. Make the necessary adjustments to your *Action Chart* before turning to **219**.

95

'What proof have we that you're not bandits in stolen uniforms?'

What can you say or do that will convince them that you speak the truth?

If you wish to say that you are a Kai Lord and that

your men are Border Rangers of Sommerlund,
turn to **259**.
If you wish to show them your Badge of Rank, turn
to **195**.

96

A tentacle smashes straight through the keel with
such force that the boat is lifted into the air and you
are thrown head over heels into the icy river.

Pick a number from the *Random Number Table*.

If the number you have picked is *0–4*, turn to **47**.
If it is *5–8*, turn to **234**.
If it is *9*, turn to **334**.

97

As you emerge from the tunnel you glimpse the
silhouette of the guards approaching. You curse
yourself for taking the wrong route; you have now
walked straight into a patrol. However, before they
can catch you, you turn and make a hasty escape.

Turn to **199**.

98

The warrior's scimitar slices the air barely inches
above your head as you drop through the trapdoor.
He attempts to follow you but is forced back by your
weapon blows. You manage to slam the trapdoor
shut and draw the bolt, locking the warrior out of the
watchtower. Wiping the grime of battle from your
stinging eyes, you run down the stairs and out of the
watchtower door.

Turn to **59**.

99

In the darkness, you fail to notice a jagged hole in the planking of the bridge. You step straight into it and crash head first to the ground, over a hundred feet below.

Your life and your mission end here.

100 – *Illustration VI (overleaf)*

An empty feeling grips your stomach as you stare upon the altar and inner sanctum of the subterranean temple. Your Kai senses burn as if every nerve in your body is screaming a warning to flee from this evil chamber. Huge braziers of molten metal encircle a black altar upon which lies fair Madelon, the daughter of Baron Vanalund. She seems to be entranced – her breathing is slow and shallow. Beyond the altar lie two massive doors, a gigantic skull engraved upon their black stone surface. Out of your view, another door opens, and a procession of red-cloaked priests enter the temple. Their heads are covered and they each carry strange amulets of black stone. They file past the altar, depositing the amulets in a circle around the young girl's body and then file out again in total silence. Then you hear the sound of a distant drumbeat; it grows louder and nearer. The measured steps of steel-shod boots resound in its wake. Barraka is approaching.

Turn to **215**.

101

You follow the tunnel for over two hours before arriving in a huge cavern. The gloomy hall is divided

VI. A procession of red-cloaked priests enter the temple

by an underground river that disappears into a wide archway in the south wall. On its opposite bank, you can just make out the shape of another passage leading to the west. A small rowing boat is beached on this side of the river and two pairs of oars are discovered behind the moss-covered boulder to which it is tied.

If you wish to row across to the other bank and take the west tunnel, turn to **343**.

If you wish to take the boat and continue south via the river, turn to **115**.

102

Your men draw their swords and advance on the strangers. The hooded men immediately raise their hands and emerge from beneath the stone canopy. One of the men drops a small earthenware flask full of clear fluid and it shatters on the hard marble floor. A search of their bodies reveals 12 Gold Crowns and enough food for 2 Meals. Make the necessary adjustments to your *Action Chart*. Around their necks they wear wooden amulets carved in the likeness of small fish.

If you possess the Kai Discipline of Healing, turn to **19**.

If you do not have this skill, turn to **339**.

103

You escape from the warrior but not before he has wounded you with his scimitar. You lose 4 ENDURANCE points.

Gasping from the pain of your wound, you manage

to pull the trapdoor shut and draw the bolt before staggering down the stairs and out through the watchtower door.

Turn to **59**.

104

Mustering all your reserves of speed and stamina you sprint towards the far side of the bridge. The blood is pounding in your ears and you pray that the locking pins will hold just long enough for you to reach safety. You are barely ten feet from the far side when the floor shudders and falls.

If you want to try to dive for the far side, turn to **303**.

If you wish to jump clear of the bridge and dive into the unknown depths of the mine shaft, turn to **342**.

105

A group of armed guards suddenly appear at the top of the stairs and command you to halt. When you hesitate, they quickly unsling crossbows from their shoulders.

If you wish to attack the guards, turn to **285**.

If you wish to raise your hands and surrender, turn to **267**.

106

The horses are a small stocky breed known as kucheks. They are named after a town and province of Vassagonia, a country many hundred of miles to the east. The bandits you encountered on the Ruanon Pike rode kucheks.

If you wish to leave Eshnar as quickly as possible, turn to **67**.

If you decide to investigate the stables, turn to **236**.

107

The bandit horseman pursues you, his lance speeding closer and closer behind you. You are running flat out and it is too late to dodge the Sommlending soldier who now stands in your way, his bow drawn ready to fire.

'Dive!' he screams at you, and instinctively you obey his bold command. Almost simultaneously, he releases the bowstring. The bandit is barely feet away when the steel-tipped arrow penetrates his visor and erupts from the rear of his helmet like a skewer through an apple. The charging horse crashes to the ground throwing its dead rider at your side. You open your mouth to shout your thanks, but before you can speak the soldier turns and hurries away to the barricade.

If you wish to follow him, turn to **59**.

(contd over)

If you wish to continue towards the watchtower, turn to **310**.

108

The leader of the tunnel guards barks an order to his men and they immediately halt in their tracks. It is obvious that they have been told not to interfere in this combat, for it seems their leader wants you all to himself.

He is wearing a tall, plumed helmet and a brilliant red sash across his chest. With one quick movement, he levels his halberd at your head and attacks.

Tunnel Guard Officer:
COMBAT SKILL 20   ENDURANCE 30

You may evade combat at any time by dashing across the bridge, and turning to **271**.
If you win the fight, turn to **28**.

109

You roll the dead bandit over with the toe of your boot, and make a quick search of his body. You discover the following items:

3 Gold Crowns
Dagger
Sword

You may take any of the above items. As you are leaving, you notice a trapdoor in the floor. Opening it, you see that it leads down to the cellar of the building.

If you wish to search the cellar, turn to **347**.
If you wish to leave the hut, turn to **258**.

110

You kick open the door and rush in. Unfortunately it is not the actor who stands before you now, but a young woman in the middle of taking her bath. After a few seconds of stunned silence, the woman begins to scream at the top of her voice, pausing only to throw at you anything that comes to hand. In a shower of hairbrushes, mirrors, combs and curses, you are driven from the coach and the door is slammed firmly in your face. Outside you find a small crowd of people who have been attracted by the noise, none of whom can speak or understand Sommlending. You find it impossible to explain your innocent mistake and, confronted by their stony stares, you are forced to abandon your search for the runaway actor.

Turn to **165**.

111

You steel yourself, mustering all your concentration for the exact moment to strike. Your warrior senses are razor-sharp; your attack is lightning fast. You lunge forward beneath the bandit's sweeping longsword, and sever the belly strap of his saddle. The saddle jerks to one side and he slips from his horse, crashing to the ground in a cloud of dirt and ash. You advance to finish him, but he is quick to recover from the fall. Leaping to his feet, he turns to face you.

If you wish to fight him, turn to **90**.
If you wish to evade combat, turn to **163**.

112

The bridge slams into the rock wall with a bone-jarring crunch.

113

Pick a number from the *Random Number Table*. If your current ENDURANCE points total is less than 10, deduct 3 from the number that you have picked.

If your current ENDURANCE points total is more than 20, add 3 to the number you have picked.

If your total score is now − 3–4, turn to **42**.
If it is 5–12, turn to **303**.

113

You enter the forest and descend the wooded hillside towards the River Xane. You have gone only a few yards when the trees become far too dense for you to be able to continue on horseback. Reluctantly, you signal to your men to dismount and continue on foot.

You soon reach the river and follow the foam-flecked water upstream. The climb takes you through a maze of wide rock terraces worn smooth by the force of the river. Then, at a point where the torrent is fed by many smaller streams, you catch sight of six bandits, stabbing at the water with their spears as it thunders along the smooth-hewn channels. On the far bank, you can see a pile of grey fish standing next to a horse-drawn wagon, which you recognize as a Sommlending cavalry wagon.

If you have reached the Kai rank of Warmarn, turn to **166**.

If you have yet to reach this level of Kai training, you can launch a surprise attack on the bandits, and turn to **14**.

If you would rather try to sneak across the river under the cover of the many large boulders that divert the watercourse, turn to **316**.

If you would rather avoid crossing here and head back the way you have just come, turn to **232**.

114

You order your men to prepare for combat and signal to one of the tavern-keeper's sons to open the doors. No sooner has he slid back the great iron bolt than the doors burst inwards. A dozen rain-drenched bandits charge into the tavern, their shields linked before them rim to rim. Your men press forward to halt their advance, hacking and stabbing whenever a head or arm presents a target, but they are forced to turn back when more bandits flood into the tavern.

A tall warrior in bright scarlet armour suddenly breaks clear of the shield wall and runs at you. His sword is raised to stab.

Bandit Warrior: COMBAT SKILL 16   ENDURANCE 25

You cannot evade combat and must fight the warrior to the death.

If you win the fight, turn to **295**.

115

As you drift beneath the arch of the southern tunnel, you pull your Kai cloak around your body and raise the hood. The ceiling is leaking and huge drops of ore-stained water rain down on your crowded boat, streaking the hair and tunics of your men a rusty brown.

You row for over a mile before eventually emerging in a small grotto. A flight of stone steps rises out of the river and ascends to an archway in the rock wall.

If you wish to land at the steps and investigate the tunnel, turn to **8**.

If you wish to continue south by the river, turn to **240**.

116

'I was hoping the King would send a large search party,' says Captain D'Val wryly, now having fully recovered from his exhaustion. 'I was beginning to tire of this town.'

You rise from your straw bed, and offer your thanks to the Captain; his brave and timely action saved you from certain death. ''Tis nothing to compare with you, Lone Wolf. Your bravery is legend. Your presence here is worth a hundred men.'

He asks you about your mission and you recount the events that have led you to this meeting; the ride south, the loss of your company, your passage through the Maaken mines and the bandits.

'Yes, the bandits – Barraka's men,' retorts D'Val, his gruff voice conveying his contempt for them and their leader. 'It seems we have both suffered at his hand. A month ago, he and his Vassagonian renegades ambushed my troop on the Ruanon Pike. We were sorely outnumbered and the fight was indeed bitter. But we broke free from them and escaped here to Ruanon. We have been beleaguered ever since and praying for help to arrive. We have enough weapons to resist them but we have barely enough food and water to survive.

You ask what has become of the people of Ruanon. 'Most are now slaves. Barraka has taken the mines and he uses the Ruanese as forced labour. Other than yourself, only one man has escaped from the mines and survived the Warhounds and the bandit snipers. That man is Baron Oren Vanalund. Come, I shall take you to him.'

D'Val leads you to the topmost chamber of the watchtower and pushes open an iron-shod door. The sight that greets you fills your heart with sorrow and pity.

Turn to **318**.

117

You soon reach a section of tunnel that is under repair. Part of the floor has subsided and a gaping hole is spanned by a rickety wooden bridge. You are tired and fail to notice that your Torch has almost burnt out. You are at the centre of the bridge when the Torch flickers and dies; you are plunged into darkness.

If you have another Torch in your Backpack, turn to **22**.

If you have no other Torch, you must try to inch your way across the bridge in total darkness. Pick a number from the *Random Number Table*. If you have the Kai Discipline of Sixth Sense or Tracking, add 3 to the number you have picked.

If your total is now *0–6*, turn to **99**.
If it is *7–12*, turn to **256**.

118

The iron door is locked. But there is a lockplate with a keyhole and a large handle upon which hangs a Whip. If you decide to take the Whip, remember to mark it on your *Action Chart* as a Backpack Item.

If you possess an Iron Key, you may open the door by turning to **308**.

If you do not possess this key or if you do not want to open the door, you may leave the chamber via a spiral staircase.

If you wish to ascend the stairs, turn to **170**.
If you wish to descend the stairs, turn to **228**.

119

'Hold your blade, Barraka. Her life is not yours for the taking!' Your words ring out above the howling wind. The renegade noble turns to face you, his laugh as piercing as your command. He advances towards you, the flame-licked dagger held high in his mailed fist. You draw your weapon and enter the temple.

If you wish to enter into combat with this warrior lord, turn to **296**.
If you wish to try to free Madelon, turn to **73**.

120

After many hours of riding you reach a highway junction. A large signpost indicates two destinations: south to Ruanon (60 miles) and east to Eshnar (40 miles).

If you wish to continue south, turn to **33**.
If you decide to go east, turn to **92**.

121

No sooner has he fallen at your feet than another line of the enemy surges forward. Your men are brave and stolid but the enemy are greater in number. You cannot hold them forever.

'Into the mine!' you shout, as the enemy pull back to regroup for another charge. But only four of your company make it to the mine; the others lie dead beneath their shields.

Turn to **248**.

122

As you raise your golden sword, the howling wind seems to rise in pitch and intensity. It claws at your mind, filling your head with terrible images of death and horror. Barraka sees you falter and strikes a cruel blow that opens a wound in your cheek. You lose 1 ENDURANCE point. But the sudden pain reawakens you to the presence of your enemy, and the combat begins.

Barraka: COMBAT SKILL 25   ENDURANCE 29

You are being attacked by a very powerful Mindblast. Unless you possess the Kai Discipline of Mindshield, your COMBAT SKILL is reduced by 4 for the duration of this combat. However, Barraka himself is a warrior who possesses formidable strength of will: he is immune to Mindblast.

If you win the combat, turn to **350**.

123

Onward and upward, you claw your way through the wooded hillside. Your throat is dry and your heart is pounding as though it is about to burst, but you dare not slacken your pace. Four hours pass before you feel certain that you have outrun the enemy.

It is nearly dusk when you chance upon a narrow steep-sided valley, carved from the hillside to afford access to a mine tunnel. For hundreds of years, the ore of the Maaken range has been the blessing and the bane of many who have ventured here to seek their fortune: men have found wealth beyond their wildest dreams but also men have perished without trace in its labryrinth of cold dark tunnels.

You examine the mine entrance. You know that if you can find a major passage, you could trace your way to Ruanon itself. At the entrance, you find a discarded wooden crate, containing six Torches and a Tinderbox. The mines are dark and you will need to use at least one Torch to light your way. You can take as many as you wish but remember each Torch counts as one Backpack Item, so be sure to make the appropriate changes to your *Action Chart*.

Enter the mines by turning to **315**.

124 – *Illustration VII*

A mantlet, a large shield on wheels, is being pushed slowly across the body-strewn battleground towards

VII.   A mantlet is being pushed across the battleground towards
the barricade

the barricade. Arrow shafts soon bristle from its thick wooden planks as D'Val's men fire their bows time and time again in an attempt to hit the shielded foe.

Suddenly a robed figure darts from behind the mantlet and levels a black staff at the barricade. He is cut down by an arrow, but not before he has let loose from his staff a guttering ball of flame. It cartwheels across the plain and explodes with a tremendous roar, hurling the bodies of defenders and shattered barricade high into the air. Through the cloud of dust and debris, you can see a line of enemy cavalry charging across the plain. They wear tall plumed helmets of polished steel and breastplates of deepest crimson. In the wake of the fireball they pour through the remains of the barricade and attack – they give no quarter. A horseman spurs his horse towards you, his lance levelled at your chest.

If you wish to stand and fight the horseman, turn to **333**.

If you wish to run back to the watchtower, turn to **107**.

A smile flickers across your face as you give the rope a hefty tug. Confidently you turn to watch your pursuers drop into the gaping mine shaft. Unfortunately the only thing to drop is the heavy portcullis that has now sealed off the entrance to the tunnel. Your enemies cackle with glee and draw their weapons to strike.

You cannot evade them and must fight them one at a time as they leap from the bridge.

Tunnel Guard Leader:
COMBAT SKILL 20   ENDURANCE 30
Tunnel Guard 1: COMBAT SKILL 18   ENDURANCE 26
Tunnel Guard 2: COMBAT SKILL 16   ENDURANCE 24

If you win, turn to **261**.

126

Darkness soon engulfs the Ruanon Pike and you are forced to stop and pitch camp. A large fire is blazing and a perimeter guard is posted to prevent any risk of a surprise attack during the night. You must now eat a Meal or lose 3 ENDURANCE points.

The night passes without incident and at dawn you break camp, continuing your ride along 'Raider's Road'.

Pick a number from the *Random Number Table*.

If the number that you have picked is 0–4, turn to **25**.

If it is 5–9, turn to **171**.

127

As you crawl from under the body of the Elix, you see the desperate struggle still raging in the chamber. Two of your men lie dead, their throats torn out by the ferocious beasts. Another is pinned beneath an Elix, his sword thrust into its side. The other ranger has reached the stairs and is desperately hacking at the head and neck of an Elix whose teeth are sunk into his foot.

There is no sign of the guards; they have been knocked backwards into the well and have fallen to a watery doom.

If you wish to help the ranger who is pinned to the
floor, turn to **178**.

If you wish to help the ranger who is fighting at the
bottom of the stairs, turn to **245**.

128

You dive towards the trapdoor but the warrior is
rushing to intercept your escape.

Pick a number from the *Random Number Table*.

If you have the Kai Discipline of Hunting, add 3 to the
number you have chosen.

If your total is now *0–4*, turn to **103**.
If it is *5–12*, turn to **98**.

129

You soon arrive at a collapsed section of the tunnel. A
wide rift has appeared in the floor and a makeshift
bridge has been thrown across it. In spite of the many
gaping holes in the bridge floor you make your way
safely to the other side.

You are hungry and must now eat a Meal or lose
3 ENDURANCE points. Make the necessary adjustments
to your *Action Chart* before turning to **309**.

130

For over an hour, you follow the river bank as it
wends its way into the foothills of the Maaken range.
The River Xane is wide and fast flowing; there are no
signs of any bridges or fords in this direction.

If you wish to return to the boathouse, turn to **68**.
If you wish to continue following the river towards
the east, turn to **331**.

131

The door is unlocked and opens out into a dimly lit tunnel. This section of the mine looks newly constructed, for the timbers are clean and the floor has yet to be worn smooth by the passage of miners and wagons. The tunnel heads south for nearly a mile before turning abruptly to the west.

Turn to **185**.

132

Your men tether their horses and follow you into the tavern. An old woman stands behind the bar, her face taut and lined as if in pain. She wears men's clothes – a shirt and checkered trousers. The tavern is empty but the tables are covered with ale mugs, many half full of beer.

If you feel uneasy about the tavern, turn to **67**.
If you wish to question the old woman, turn to **287**.

133

The bandits close on you from three sides and move in for the kill. They attack simultaneously and you must fight all three as one enemy.

Bandit Patrol: COMBAT SKILL 18   ENDURANCE 35

You may evade combat at any time by running towards Ruanon. Turn to **307**.

If you lose any ENDURANCE points during this combat, turn to **17**.

If you win the combat without losing any ENDURANCE points, turn to **265**.

134

You soon arrive at the entrance to a mine. Two sets of footprints disappear into the gloom of the tunnel and, judging by their shape and size, they were made by two of your missing scouts. You shout into the mine but there is no reply to your call.

If you wish to enter the mine, turn to **91**.

If you decide to call off your search, return along the hill track and turn to **191**.

135

The bleak, treeless Wildlands offer no cover in which you can hide from the bandit hordes. They out-number your men by four to one and the life and death of your entire company now depends on your decision.

If you wish to counter-attack the bandits in the hope that your bold action will scare them off, turn to **284**.

If you wish to split your company, detaching a group of ten rangers to follow you whilst sending the remainder off towards the west in the hope of luring the bulk of the bandit horde away to the Durncrag mountains, turn to **211**.

If you wish to head south at the gallop, to try to reach the shelter of the Ruanon forest before the bandits close in, turn to **30**.

136

The injured man is in a state of shock; his left arm is completely smashed above and below the elbow and many of his ribs are broken.

If you have the Kai Discipline of Healing, turn to **313**.
If you do not possess this skill, turn to **216**.

137

All around the barricade the enemy are retreating in disorder; bandit war-horns announce the withdrawal, exhorting their defeated warriors to flee the battlefield. A jubilant Captain D'Val emerges from the war-smoke, his eyes shining like jewels beneath the rim of his battered helmet. 'We have triumphed, Lone Wolf. We have vanquished the foe!'

All around you, the Captain's men are rebuilding the barricade and tending to their wounded comrades. It sorrows you to see Sommlending dead, but you take heart at how few they are beside the enemy's losses.

The Captain ushers you to the watchtower where your wounds are cleaned and dressed with Laumspur. The herbs restore 6 ENDURANCE points.

'We have beaten this foe but I fear that it is but a temporary reprieve,' says the Captain, his face now composed and sombre. 'The sacrifice of Baron Vanalund's daughter must be stopped if we are to avoid catastrophe, for our strength will not avail us against a foe freshly risen from the grave.'

The words of the verse flood into your mind and a chill runs down your spine as you realize what may lie ahead. In three days' time, when the moon is full, Barraka will sacrifice the Baron's daughter at the buried temple of Maaken, a sacrifice that will unleash the dead of Maakengorge – the chasm of doom. You know you must prevent the sacrifice.

Turn to **12**.

138

You are halfway down the ramp when a guard turns to face you. He blinks and rubs his bloodshot eyes in disbelief. You seize your advantage and sprint at the man, hoping to reach him before he fully comes to his senses. Just as he begins to shout, you strike and send him tumbling over the edge of the ramp. The other guard draws his sword and staggers to his feet. He is obviously very drunk and is maddened by your attack – he springs towards you like a rabid dog.

Drunken Guard: COMBAT SKILL 13   ENDURANCE 29

You can evade combat at any time by running into the tunnel on this level. Turn to **81**.

If you win the combat, turn to **152**.

139

You send three of your men into the valley with orders to scout the highway and its forested borders for bandits. Before the scouts leave, you remind them to report back within two hours.

You are hungry and you must now eat a Meal or lose 3 ENDURANCE points. In spite of their fatigue, your men are now alert and ready for action; for it has been over three hours since your scouts departed and not one of them has yet returned.

If you wish to send three more scouts into the wooded valley, turn to **206**.

If you wish to wait until dawn before you investigate their disappearance, turn to **330**.

If you decide that it is far too dangerous to stay here, you can still ride east towards the town of Eshnar by turning to **92**.

140

Dusk soon enshrouds the beleaguered outpost of Ruanon and you use the cover of darkness to cross the body-strewn plain towards the south. An old highway trails off to Maaken but it is choked with Vassagonian warriors. They stand about in sullen groups, tending their wounded and brooding on their defeat; however, even demoralized and dejected, they are still a deadly foe. It will be too dangerous to risk passing through their ranks, so you must use the forest to conceal your passage.

If you wish to venture through the trees to the right of the highway, turn to **70**.

If you wish to pass through the trees to the left, turn to **314**.

141

You have not ridden far when a storm cloud breaks directly overhead and torrential rain crashes down. Within minutes, the dry and dusty highway is trans-

142

formed into a quagmire. It will be impossible to set up camp in this storm, so you resolve to continue to ride all night in the hope that the storm will soon pass. During your night ride you must eat a Meal or lose 3 ENDURANCE points.

By morning the rain has ceased, but you and your men are now very tired from the ordeal.

Turn to **253**.

142 – *Illustration VIII*

Dawn arrives, rainswept and gloom-laden. A pall of drizzle hangs over the ghost city and the gruesome discord of the wailing winds of Maakengorge make you feel uneasy. You watch and wait, your Kai cloak drawn close about your shoulders to keep out the chill, damp air.

It was here, during the Age of the Black Moon, that King Ulnar of Sommerlund killed the mightiest of the Darklords – Lord Vashna. In mortal combat upon the very brink of the abyss, the Darklord was slain by the Sommerswerd. It is said that his death cry when he fell will echo through the gorge until the day he rises to wreak his vengeance on Sommerlund and the House of Ulnar. Your stomach contracts at the thought that this could be that very day.

For five hours you observe and take in every detail of the ruined city. The first line of the strange verse keeps repeating itself in your mind. 'When the full moon shines o'er the temple deep . . .' The temple must be underground and there must be an entrance to it – but where?

VIII. The crypt door is guarded by two Vassagonian warriors

143–144

You study every crack in the broken ground and eliminate all but two possibilities; a crypt door guarded by two Vassagonian warriors, and a flight of marble steps descending into the earth between two columns of fractured pillars.

> If you wish to try to enter the temple through the guarded crypt door, turn to **183**.
> If you wish to try to enter the temple via the unguarded marble stairs, turn to **270**.

143

No matter how hard you strike the prop, it will not fall. Suddenly your pursuers charge out of the gloomy tunnel and attack you.

Although there are only two pursuers, others are close behind. You must fight them one at a time.

Tunnel Guard 1: COMBAT SKILL 16   ENDURANCE 22
Tunnel Guard 2: COMBAT SKILL 15   ENDURANCE 21

> If you manage to kill the first guard, you can evade further combat by turning to **87**.
> If you kill both guards in combat, turn to **230**.

144

You vault over the edge of the wagon and run, little dreaming of what lies ahead. The causeway wall is high and you cannot stop yourself in time from falling over the edge. You crash head first into a quarry over one hundred feet below, glimpsing the horrified expression of your unknown friend as you fall.

Your life and your mission end here.

145

The tunnel descends for miles into solid rock. You are occasionally startled by unexpected swarms of glowing mine flies or fluttering bats swooping out of the darkness, attracted by your body heat.

You eventually reach a chamber where a small wooden hut has been built against the wall. You are now desperately tired and in need of sleep.

If you wish to rest in the hut, turn to **322**.
If you wish to press on regardless of fatigue, turn to **162**.

146

The bandit tumbles into the rushing water and disappears from view. You leap from stone to stone in pursuit of the two bandits who have survived the ambush and who are now scurrying off towards the far bank to alert the other bandits inside the wagon. As the bandits emerge from the wagon, to your horror, you notice they are all armed with bows which they train upon your advancing rangers with deadly precision.

As you shout a warning, an iron-tipped shaft creases your scalp and you are knocked backwards into the swift dark waters of the River Xane.

Turn to **272**.

147

The guard hears you approaching and spins round. He stares at you aghast and unsheathes his sword. Due to the surprise of your attack, you may ignore any ENDURANCE points lost in the first round of combat.

Bridge Guard: COMBAT SKILL 14   ENDURANCE 23

If you win the combat, turn to **280**.

148 – *Illustration IX*

'To me! To me!' Captain D'Val's voice booms out above the battle noise. 'Rally to me, Sommlending.'

The brave Captain draws about him a shielded wedge of soldiers and charges into the flank of the horsemen. They reel and buckle as the shield-wedge hews its way through their company. A Vassagonian herald, his crimson armour torn and his face smeared with blood, breaks free from the battle and sounds the retreat. You watch as the surviving bandits spur their mounts to the gallop, desperate to escape through the ragged hole in the barricade. Gripped by panic and fatigue, they ride through their own foot soldiers who are advancing to support them. The infantry falter and collapse as the cavalry ride them down.

Captain D'Val leads his men to the barricade and directs a lethal volley of arrows into the shattered

IX.   A Vassagonian herald breaks free from the battle and
sounds the retreat

infantry. It is the last straw. They throw down their weapons and flee from the clouds of arrows raining down on them from out of the smoke-filled sky.

A battle-cry, proud and strident pursues them across the plain: 'For Sommerlund, for Sommerlund!'

Turn to **137**.

149

A dreadful feeling of guilt sweeps over you as you recognize these amulets. They are the symbols of a holy order of monks known as 'The Redeemers', a silent order devoted to pilgrimage, prayer and the healing arts.

You curse your hasty action and carefully replace the amulets around the necks of the holy men.

Turn to **188**.

150

The tracks lead to the overgrown entrance of a mine tunnel. You peer into the gloomy passage to see that many of the beams and props that once supported the roof have now collapsed. Mounds of moss-covered earth litter the tunnel floor and a rivulet of ore-stained water trickles a winding course around them.

The hoof prints end at the entrance but two sets of footprints continue into the mine.

If you wish to send your men in search of the missing horses, turn to **164**.

If you wish to follow the footprints into the mine, turn to **288**.

If you wish to call off the search, you can return along the hill track by turning to **6**.

151

The floor of the tunnel is covered with the decaying remains of rodents. The sound of cracking bones makes you wince with disgust as you and your men step gingerly through the foul-smelling debris.

You reach a section where the tunnel curves abruptly to the east, revealing the reflections of torchlight on the rough stone walls. A quick check ahead confirms your suspicions; two armour-clad warriors stand guard at a well sunk into a torchlit chamber.

If you wish to signal to your men to attack the guards, turn to **320**.

If you wish to try to lure them into the tunnel and capture them alive, turn to **197**.

152

A quick search of the body reveals the following items:

> Sword
> 6 Gold Crowns
> Enough food for two Meals
> Brass Key

You may take any of these items but remember to mark them on your *Action Chart*.

As you turn to enter the tunnel, a guard appears on the ramp below. He sees you and sounds the alarm by blowing on a war-horn strung around his neck. You do not stay to witness the response to his alarm signal. With its sound ringing in your ears you escape into the tunnel at a run.

Turn to **81**.

153

You release the shaft and it whistles towards the bandit leader; but he sees its deadly approach and raises his polished steel shield. Your heart sinks as the arrow is turned aside; it shatters harmlessly against the watchtower wall. Before you can fire again, the bow is suddenly kicked from your grasp. You are confronted by an armoured warrior. He stands above you on the barricade wall and you cannot evade his attack.

Vassagonian Warrior:
COMBAT SKILL 17   ENDURANCE 26

You sheathed your weapon in order to use the bow but unfortunately the warrior attacks before you can draw it to defend yourself. Therefore you must deduct 4 points from your COMBAT SKILL for the first two rounds of combat. If you are still alive by the third round, you manage to unsheathe your weapon and retaliate.

If you win the combat, turn to **174**.

154

When you are certain that the bandits are no longer in pursuit, you halt to rally your tired and tattered company. Only ten men have survived the battle, the rest have either been captured or been killed before they could escape. With the highway to Sommerlund now cut off by bandits, you have no choice but to continue southwards.

Pick a number from the *Random Number Table*.

If the number you have picked is *0–2*, turn to **120**.
If it is *3–9*, turn to **51**.

155

Beyond the approaching Warhound pack, you can see that a dozen bandit archers are closing in. If you were to survive the rending jaws of the Warhounds, the archers would be sure to pick you off with ease. Without wasting a second, you turn towards Ruanon and run as fast as your legs will carry you.

Turn to **225**.

156

The tunnel soon arrives at the base of a mine shaft where a ladder is fixed to the wall. This ascends to another tunnel thirty feet above, which disappears into the west wall. There is no other exit from the shaft.

If you wish to climb the ladder to the level above, turn to **212**.
If you decide to retrace your steps back to the previous chamber and take the south tunnel, turn to **101**.

157

You are now so tired that you are forced to stop and sleep. Many hours pass before you awake totally refreshed. Restore 1 ENDURANCE point and continue your exploration of the tunnel.

Turn to **309**.

158

Your stomach turns as the boat lurches forward into space. You tumble for what seems like an eternity before hitting deep water head first. The impact is so sudden and so hard that you are concussed and slip into unconsciousness. You lose 3 ENDURANCE points.

When you awake, you find yourself lying face down in mud and gravel. Your head is pounding and your lungs feel as if they are on fire. You have lost your Backpack and all that it contained. Although your vision is hazy and blurred, you are quick to realize that you are alone. No trace of your men or your boat remain. Make the necessary adjustments to your *Action Chart* by turning to **219**.

159

You lie with your face pressed close to the crop roots, your breath held and your nerves stretched as taut as bowstrings, waiting for the patrol to pass.

Hundreds of minute creatures busily file up and down the yellowed stalks. Your whole body begins to prickle as you imagine they are swarming up your legs, up your sleeves and down the neck of your tunic. When a trickle of sweat runs down your cheek, you nearly cry out and reveal your hiding place.

The bandits amble past barely inches from where you hide, totally oblivious to your presence. When you are sure they are no longer on the track, you jump up and frantically scratch at your itching skin. To your horror, you discover that your legs are covered with crawling insects feasting on your blood. Ripping your clothes off, you empty them from your boots and scrape them from your skin before hurrying off along the track. The blood-sucking insects have robbed you of 2 ENDURANCE points.

Turn to **204**.

160

An escort of five rangers accompanies you along the twisting narrow track that leads to the hut. The rough stone walls are covered with a damp moss into which is set a curious oval door. There are no windows. You have dismounted and are approaching the door when suddenly a man's voice calls from inside the hut: 'Come in, Lone Wolf, I've been expecting you.'

If you wish to open the door and enter, turn to **84**.

If you wish to draw your weapon and kick open the door, turn to **205**.

If you wish to send your rangers into the hut, turn to **306**.

161

Raising the hood of your Kai cloak, you crouch in the bottom of an empty ore wagon and wait with bated breath. Through a gap in the wood you can see a haggard procession of men shuffling towards you. An escort of bandit warriors pushes them forward, beating any who falter or slip out of line. You feel a sudden jolt as your wagon is pushed along the tunnel and glance up to see a sweat-streaked face peering down at you. 'Run left when I say "Go",' whispers the face, then disappears over the edge of the wagon.

As the wagon emerges from the tunnel, sunlight suddenly floods over you. Through the crack you can now see your destination; the wagons are being shunted on to a timber gantry where the track ends some fifty feet above a huge mound of ore. Your observations are cut short by a hissed command: 'Go!'

If you wish to leap from the wagon and run to the left, turn to **27**.

If you wish to jump from the wagon and run to the right, turn to **144**.

If you decide to ignore the command and stay where you are, turn to **294**.

162

Two mine tunnels lead out of the chamber. One heads towards the west, the other towards the south.

If you wish to go west, turn to **214**.
If you wish to go south, turn to **117**.

163

You turn and run from the Vassagonian, but trip over a broken wagon wheel and tumble to the ground. You hear the warrior's malicious laugh as he draws back his sword to strike, but the laugh suddenly changes to a ghastly howl.

You watch him slump to the ground, a Sommlending arrow deep in the nape of his neck.

Turn to **249**.

164

Suddenly, the shrill blast of a war-horn makes your blood freeze. Red-clad bandit warriors suddenly leap from the dense foliage and charge towards your men. The odds are against you, for you are outnumbered by at least three to one. There may be no escape from this deadly ambush.

If you wish to rally your men to stand and fight, turn to **299**.

If you decide to order a hasty retreat into the mine, turn to **52**.

165

You return to the troubadours' stage in time for a meal that has been prepared by your hosts. The steaming broth smells most appetising.

If you wish to accept the meal, turn to **319**.

If you decline the food, you must now eat a Meal from your Backpack or lose 3 ENDURANCE points. Turn to **13**.

166

You sense that the wagon is full of sleeping bandits. Should they awake before you cross the river undetected or before you silence all six of the bandits who are fishing, you and your men will be hard pressed to avoid death or capture. You decide that the risks are too great to attempt a crossing here, and signal to your men to follow you eastwards.

Turn to **232**.

167

To your delight you discover a miner's Backpack and a Shovel lying in the bottom of the mine wagon. Inside the Backpack is enough food for one Meal. You slip the Backpack over your shoulders before attempting to climb the steep service tunnel. Make the appropriate adjustments to your *Action Chart*, and turn to **185**.

168 – *Illustration X*

You break open the two halves of your Kalte Firesphere and hold the flaming hemispheres high as you advance deeper into the vault. You gasp as you spot a hideous black-skinned creature perched on a rail near the ceiling. Dull satanic eyes follow your every move and its mouth opens and closes, shouting silent curses. Suddenly, it glides down from its perch and attacks.

If you possess the Sommerswerd, turn to **34**.
If you do not possess this Special Item, turn to **85**.

169

As you part the dense foliage, you suddenly topple headlong over the edge of a steep drop and fall with a

X.   Dull, satanic eyes follow your every move

crash on to a wide forest track below. Less than ten feet away kneels a bandit examining the hoof of his horse, and prising out a sharp stone from the animal's shoe with a long curved dagger. The noise of your fall alerts him and he turns with his weapon raised for attack.

Bandit Warrior: COMBAT SKILL 16   ENDURANCE 24

If you win the combat, you notice that a group of bandits are closing in from the north. You spot them just in time to make a hasty escape.

Turn to **123**.

170

You climb the spiral stairs for over five minutes before reaching the next level. Here, a tunnel leads off towards the south. You march along the dank passage until you reach a point where it veers sharply to the west. A little further on, a staircase descends to your right.

If you wish to descend the staircase, turn to **228**.
If you wish to continue along the passage, turn to **221**.

171

Mile after mile you ride across the flat and desolate landscape surrounding the Ruanon Pike. Yet in spite of the uninspiring view, your men seem in fine spirits. They sing rousing marching songs to relieve the tedium of the journey, and help to allay fears of what may lie ahead. During the afternoon, storm clouds gather above the peaks of the Durncrag mountains to the west, and the roll of distant thunder warns of imminent rain.

It is late afternoon when your scouts sight a coaching tavern on the highway ahead. It is a large stone building that has been fortified.

If you wish to stop at the tavern for the night, turn to **63**.

If you decide to brave a possible storm and continue to ride south, turn to **141**.

172

You recognize the eastern accent in their voices. They are Vassagonian bandit warriors. There are at least four of them in the room beyond and they are discussing what to do about an intruder in the mines. You decide that discretion is by far the better part of valour and return to the gallery. You make sure that you are not being followed and enter the wagon tunnel in the west wall.

Turn to **55**.

173

The wooden pillar is stout and firm; it will take a heavy blow to dislodge it.

If you possess the Sommerswerd, turn to **275**.

If you do not possess the Sommerswerd pick a number from the *Random Number Table*. If you possess either a Pick or a Shovel, add 2 to the number you have picked.

If your total is now *0–6*, turn to **143**.
If it is *7–11*, turn to **179**.

174

More enemy warriors are clambering across the shattered barricade towards you. You throw down your bow and run to a large water cask, which is being defended by a stout Sommlending sergeant. The ground around the cask is carpeted with enemy dead.

'Shoot the leader!' you command, pointing towards the enemy officer. The sergeant aims and fires his bow with one swift and fluid movement. The arrow arcs through the smoke-blackened sky and pierces the officer's shiny breastplate. Slowly his cruel eyes flicker and close, and he slips from his saddle with the arrow lodged deep in his heart.

Turn to **148**.

175

You have covered less than a mile when disaster strikes. Without warning, a ranger in front of you lets out a piercing cry; a disc of razor sharp steel has sunk into his chest. More of the deadly discs cut the air, whistling past you on all sides. Before you all fall prey to the hidden assassins, you lead your men away at a gallop.

When you finally rein in your sweating horse, you are more than two miles from the scene of the ambush and only four of your men remain at your side. Your halt must be brief, for the enemy may already be in pursuit. With the terrible sound of the deadly steel discs still ringing in your ears, you lead the remnants of your company southwards along the highway.

Turn to **297**.

176

With a bone-jarring crunch, your horse crashes into the flank of a bandit steed, and you are hurled head over heels to the ground. You are stunned by the shock of impact and fail to see the blade that bites into your shoulder. Lose 3 ENDURANCE points before turning to face your attacker. You cannot evade combat and must fight your adversary to the death.

Bandit Warrior: COMBAT SKILL 17   ENDURANCE 25

If you win, turn to **7**.

177

You have taken just one step into the cavern when a blow on the back of your head knocks you senseless. You were seen at the junction by two guards who prepared this ambush for you. Your equipment is taken and your unconscious body bound by Barraka's men who throw you into a cell.

You are unable to stop the sacrifice. When the time comes for your cell door to open, it is the bony hand of a skeleton that turns the key.

Your life and your mission end here.

178

You drag the loathsome creature away from the ranger only to find that the man is dead. The Elix has already sunk its needle-like teeth into the poor man's heart.

Grabbing your weapon you turn to help the other man who is now being attacked by two of the giant war-cats. A third Elix pounces at you as you run across the chamber, but you strike it in mid-air, sending it tumbling into the well.

Turn to **245**.

179

The prop begins to splinter and break in two. A shudder runs through the floor, making you stumble and fall, but you quickly regain your footing. As you sprint to safety, a deluge of earth and stone pours into the tunnel behind. A shock wave from the blast hits you squarely in the back and flattens you to the floor; the air is choked with dust. You stagger to your feet and press on, but it takes you half an hour to reach a section of the tunnel where the air is clear and still and the torches are still burning.

Turn to **335**.

180

On the far side of the boathouse, a narrow slipway descends to a door at river level. One of your men hurries over and raises the stout drawbar while the others carry the rowing boat down the ramp. You push off and clamber aboard, emerging from the boathouse with such a jolt that you are thrown forward in a heap. By the time you have disentangled yourselves, the boat is firmly in the grip of the river current. You grab an oar and fight to keep the boat in the centre of the rushing water as it speeds on its course through the foothills of the Maaken range. But no sooner has the boat been brought under control than you are confronted by an unexpected hazard: ahead of you the river suddenly disappears into the rockface beneath a massive granite ledge. It is too late to avoid being swept into the inky black cavern and as you glide into the darkness you prepare yourself for any hidden dangers that may lurk inside.

Turn to **241**.

181

The twang of the sniper's bow and the hiss of an arrow are the last sounds that you hear in this world. The shaft punctures your skull and you die instantly.

Your life and your mission end here.

182

The wagons are drawn into a circle and you set up camp inside. A ranger is posted to patrol the perimeter. The troubadours construct a small stage on to which strides Yesu. He calls for silence before announcing the title of their play, 'The Brave Warriors of Sommerlund', a choice that meets with the hearty approval of your men.

During the performance, you notice something very odd; not only is one of the actors using a real sword, but it is a type of sword only issued to officers of the Sommlending cavalry. After the play you approach the man to question him about the sword. He looks at you nervously and makes a dash for the darkness of the perimeter wagons.

> If you wish to give chase and have either the Kai Discipline of Tracking or Hunting, turn to **332**.
>
> If you do not possess these skills but still wish to give chase, turn to **58**.
>
> If you decide to let him go, return to your men by turning to **165**.

You manage to reach a tangle of briars growing near the crypt door, and from here you can observe the Vassagonian guards undetected. More soldiers appear on horseback, riding into Maaken from the north. They dismount and approach the door.

'Password!' shout the crypt guards.
'Lohn,' reply the soldiers. The door opens and they are allowed to enter.

Armed with the password, you decide to try to enter in the same way. Keeping the hood of your cloak

raised and your Sommlending features in shadow, you walk boldly towards the guards.

Pick a number from the *Random Number Table*.

If you have the Kai Discipline of Camouflage, add 4 to the number you have picked.

If your total is now *0–6*, turn to **198**.
If it is *7–13*, turn to **338**.

184
You are barely ten yards from the enemy when they fire. Miraculously you are not hit but you must now fight alone, as three of your men lie dead and the other can no longer fight; a bolt has shattered his wrist. As you attack, the fierce warriors discard their empty crossbows and draw their swords, and you find yourself being pushed back to the bridge by six angry swordsmen.

If you wish to fight them, turn to **202**.
If you wish to dive over the parapet of the bridge to avoid them, turn to **342**.

185
You are hungry and must now eat a Meal or lose 3 ENDURANCE points. You then continue along the tunnel, which runs for several miles before eventually arriving at a long, deserted gallery.

Turn to **40**.

186
The Vassagonian bandits break cover and charge, and you give the order to fire. A cloud of arrows sweeps down upon the armour-clad men, the

hardened tips penetrating their scarlet plate. The first wave of assailants tumbles and falls; the second wave falters. Another volley forces them back and they retreat to the ruins to reorganize themselves.

Here and there, groups of bandit warriors have survived the hail of death and reached the barricade. Most are slain as they try to enter, but a small and determined section of their boldest fighters have broken through close to where you stand. Suddenly, a thick-bodied warrior with oily black hair tied in a knot at the back of his scarred head, leaps on to the wagon and attacks you.

Vassagonian Warrior:
COMBAT SKILL 18   ENDURANCE 25

You can evade combat at any time by jumping from the wagon. Turn to **66**.
If you win the fight, turn to **243**.

187

Discarding your torch as you emerge into the early morning sun, you signal to your men to gather round. Only a small fraction of your original company remains, and you must now decide the best course of action. However, as you are about to address them you are rudely interrupted.

Turn to **164**.

188

You order your men to prepare graves for the two corpses before returning to the shelter of the marble canopy. You are hungry and must now eat a Meal or lose 3 ENDURANCE points. You mount guard around the ruined temple and preparations are made for some much needed sleep.

Turn to **233**.

189

You try to row the shattered boat towards the far bank, but as the oars dip below the surface they are wrenched from your grasp. Wide-eyed with horror, you watch as the ranger is dragged screaming into the dark river by a thick slimy tentacle. Suddenly, there is a tremendous crack as another tentacle punches its way up through the hull. The attack is so violent that the rowing boat is lifted into the air and you tumble head over heels into the icy water.

Pick a number from the *Random Number Table*.

If the number you have picked is *0–4*, turn to **234**.
If it is *5–9*, turn to **47**.

190

You emerge from the tunnel, curse your delay, and press on along the other passage as quickly as possible.

Turn to **335**.

191

You soon reach a junction where the track meets the main highway. Abandoned at the side of the road is a burnt-out wagon.

If you wish to examine the wagon, turn to **337**.
If you decide to ignore the wreck, you can continue your ride south along the highway, by turning to **297**.

192

You are less than five feet from the door when a bandit warrior comes rushing in. Instinctively, you step aside but not in time to avoid the serated tip of his halberd. The cold steel sinks into your chest and you stare down in horror as blood begins to flow and pain spreads through your body. Your wound is fatal and you die within seconds of hitting the floor.

Your life and your mission end here.

193 – *Illustration XI*

The snarling Warhounds bound towards the barricade, their gaping eyes glowing crimson in the light of battle. Leaping from the bodies of the dead and dying, they launch themselves at the Sommlending defenders. All around you, soldiers are being torn from the line, bowled over by the leaping Warhounds. You back away as a howling dog crashes through the wall of sacks and barrels, but before it has risen you move swiftly forward and despatch it with one blow to the head. Another Warhound claws your back and pitches you forward into the collapsed barricade, but before you can free yourself, yet two more dogs have sunk their fangs into your leg.

Vassagonian Warhounds:
COMBAT SKILL 17   ENDURANCE 30

If you are still alive after two rounds of combat, turn to **311**.

194

You are winded by the blow to your chest and flung backwards into the icy cold water. You surface, but

XI. The snarling Warhounds bound towards the barricade

195

barely in time to catch a breath before a tentacle coils around your legs and drags you down.

Pick a number from the *Random Number Table*, and note this number down in the margin of your *Action Chart*. (In this case 0 = 10 instead of zero). This number represents the number of combat rounds that you can endure underwater before you begin to lose additional ENDURANCE points due to lack of oxygen. If you have the Kai Discipline of Mind Over Matter, you can add 2 to the number you have picked.

Giant Meresquid: COMBAT SKILL 16   ENDURANCE 37

Fight this combat in the normal way. If the fight lasts longer than the number of rounds you can endure underwater, you will lose an additional 2 ENDURANCE points for every round of combat thereafter due to lack of oxygen.

If you win the combat, turn to **32**.

195

You hear the thud of a heavy drawbar sliding back and a burly man dressed in a leather jerkin appears at the tavern door. 'Welcome to my humble inn, my lord. Pardon my suspicion, but this is a very danger-ous area; one mistake can cost us our lives.'

You signal to your men to stable their horses and you follow the innkeeper into his tavern. The bar looks more like an armoury than a drinking hall. Quivers of arrows stand beside each of the iron-studded window shutters and racks of spears line the far wall. The place is deserted except for three young men who all bear a strong resemblance to the tavern-keeper. One of them has his head swathed in bandages.

You ask the tavern-keeper how much he will charge for your men to billet here tonight, and are quite surprised to hear his reply. 'Nothing,' he says, moving tables aside so that your rangers can sleep upon the tavern floor. 'Your presence here tonight will be worth more than gold to us. We've been attacked by bandits every night since the last full moon.'

As the last of your men return from the stables, the doors are closed and barred. It has started to rain and your men seem greatly relieved to be inside where it is warm and dry.

If you wish to question the tavern-keeper about the nature of the bandit raids, turn to **239**.

If you wish to question him about any news that he may have heard about Ruanon in the last month, then turn to **266**.

If you do not wish to question the man further, you can prepare for a night's sleep and turn to **324**.

196

A bolt of lightning gashes the stormy sky, illuminating the figures of the bandits as they creep into the stables. Crouching on the balcony, you signal to your men to prepare themselves. Dropping on to the stable roof, you discover to your dismay that the clay tiles are wafer-thin and splinter beneath your weight; you crash straight through the flimsy roof into the hay below. Luckily you are unharmed by the fall and quickly regain your feet, but a bandit stands barely inches from your face, his sword raised to strike.

Bandit Warrior: COMBAT SKILL 16   ENDURANCE 23

You cannot evade combat.

If you win, turn to **217**.

197

You toss a rock along the tunnel to attract the guards' attention. It works! Within seconds you can hear footsteps approaching. You attack. The guards barely have time to gasp and your men leap out of the darkness and overpower them. Once disarmed, their hands are tied and they are herded back into the well chamber.

If you wish to search them, turn to **268**.
If you wish to question them, turn to **76**.
If you wish to leave them and continue on your way, turn to **64**.

198

The guards are not fooled by your bravado – they draw their weapons and attack. You must fight them as one enemy.

Crypt Guards: COMBAT SKILL 18   ENDURANCE 30

If you win the combat, turn to **229**.

199

You soon enter a chamber divided by a deep mine shaft. Spanning the shaft is a wooden bridge at the entrance of which a swarthy warrior stands guard. He has been alerted by the screams of your pursuers, and as soon as he sees you, he runs towards a rope that hangs from the ceiling, leaving the bridge unguarded. Your pursuers are nearly upon you.

If you wish to sprint across the bridge, turn to **271**.

If you wish to attack the guard to prevent him from reaching the rope, turn to **56**.

200

The trees are alive with bandit patrols, but your quick wits and Kai skills prevent you from being seen by them. Eventually you reach the edge of the copse. You find yourself staring out across an expanse of open plain towards Ruanon. The sight that lies before you is very disquieting.

Much of the mining town has been burnt to the ground. The blackened ruins of what were once shops, cottages and taverns are now little more than smouldering mounds of charcoal. You are beginning to fear the worst, that Ruanon has been totally destroyed, when a gentle breeze clears the haze of woodsmoke hanging like a grey curtain over the ruins. Inside the perimeter of ruined buildings, a barricade has been thrown up around a tower of stone. Above the tower a tattered flag still flies bringing renewed hope; it is the sun-flag of Sommerlund edged with a band of white braid – the cavalry standard of the King's Guard Regiment.

The sudden crack of a twig makes you freeze. You glance behind to see three bandits creeping through the trees towards you. The wide steel tips of their spears glint. They seem to be coated with a clear, sticky fluid.

If you possess the Kai Discipline of Hunting *or* if you have ever visited Gorn Cove, turn to **45**.
If you wish to fight the bandits, turn to **133**.
If you wish to evade them, you must run across the open plain towards Ruanon – eight hundred yards away. Turn to **307**.

201

The fungi are soft and dry and they taste dreadful! You retch and choke as the dry, powdery fungi absorbs all the saliva in your mouth. You are hit by waves of nausea that make you panic, and desperately you claw at your tongue trying to scrape the fungi from your mouth.

Turn to **65**.

202

There are six heavily armed guards and you must fight them one at a time.

Guard 1: COMBAT SKILL 18   ENDURANCE 23
Guard 2: COMBAT SKILL 15   ENDURANCE 24
Guard 3: COMBAT SKILL 15   ENDURANCE 21
Guard 4: COMBAT SKILL 16   ENDURANCE 25
Guard 5: COMBAT SKILL 14   ENDURANCE 24
Guard 6: COMBAT SKILL 14   ENDURANCE 22

You can evade combat at any time by leaping from the bridge. Turn to **342**.
If you win the combat, turn to **237**.

203

As the guard falls dead at your feet, you spin around in time to see three of your pursuers enter the chamber. They are clad in heavy armour and each of them carries a vicious-looking halberd.

If you wish to fight them, turn to **108**.
If you wish to escape across the bridge, turn to **271**.

204

You bypass a village with orange-wood cabins and stone walls, and climb through the tall fields towards a wooded ridge. Beyond the ridge, you enter thick forest and discover a bubbling freshwater stream.

You drink deeply and realize how hungry you are. You must eat a Meal here or lose 3 ENDURANCE points.

As night falls you reach the city of Maaken. The gaunt, weed-infested ruins of this shattered city are spread like a vast graveyard and bathed in the eerie light of a near-full moon. A sound fills the air like the wailing of lost souls; it is the cry of Maakengorge.

It has been nearly two days since you last slept and fatigue begins to overwhelm you. Drawing your Kai cloak about your shoulders, you settle down to sleep; you will need all your strength for the daunting task that lies ahead.

Turn to **142**.

205

The oval door crashes inwards and a cloud of dust billows out of the hut.

'I am alone,' says a voice. 'You have nothing to fear from me.'

Tightening your grip on your weapon, you cautiously enter the stone hut.

Turn to **84**.

206

As the first light of dawn breaks over the eastern horizon, you scan the mist-shrouded highway for any sign of life. None of your scouts have returned and your remaining four men are visibly anxious. With marauding bandit hordes to the north, hostile mountains to the west and a two-day ride to the nearest town to the east, your choice of action is limited.

If you wish to enter the valley by the highway, turn to **82**.

If you wish to enter the valley under the cover of the forest, turn to **226**.

207

You snatch an arrow from a quiver hanging on the wall, and draw the bowstring taut to your lips. A bandit horseman races across the plain with a javelin held high in his hand. His quarry is a wounded Sommlending soldier, who has fallen from the barricade and lies on the plain, unarmed and helpless. The bandit is poised to throw his javelin when you loose your arrow.

Pick a number from the *Random Number Table*.

If you possess the Kai Discipline of Weaponskill (any weapon), add 2 to the number you have picked.

If your total is now *0–4*, turn to **336**.
If it is *5–11*, turn to **218**.

208

You have run less than twenty yards when you reach the end of the tunnel; a solid rockface. The passage has only recently been excavated and you are now trapped in a dead-end. You hear the footsteps of your pursuers and turn to face them, knowing only too well that your only chances of survival now rest on your ability to be able to fight your way out of this trap and make your way back to the junction where you can take the left-hand tunnel.

Tunnel Guard 1: COMBAT SKILL 15   ENDURANCE 25
Tunnel Guard 2: COMBAT SKILL 15   ENDURANCE 24

Tunnel Guard 3: COMBAT SKILL 14   ENDURANCE 22

If you kill all three guards, turn to **199**.

209 – *Illustration XII*

The lance has torn through your cloak and pitched you on to your back. You scramble to your feet in time to see the horseman discard his splintered lance and draw a curved broadsword. A wicked smile spreads across his grim features, exposing a jagged line of blackened teeth. He spits out his battle-cry and spurs his horse towards you once more.

If you have reached the Kai rank of Aspirant or higher, turn to **111**.

If you have yet to reach this level of Kai training, turn to **43**.

210

You have a very uneasy feeling about this town. So far you have only seen women and children shuffling along the street; there has been no sign of any men whatsoever. The inhabitants all seem nervous and avoid looking you directly in the eye. Instinct tells you to turn around and leave as quickly as possible.

If you wish to follow your instincts, turn to **67**.

If you wish to press on regardless of your instincts, you can investigate the tavern by turning to **132**.

If you wish to continue along the street, turn to **301**.

211

Your tactics have worked. The bandits ignore your small group of horsemen and pursue the others

XII.   He spits out his battle cry and spurs his horse towards you
once more

towards the west. Once they reach the wooded foot-hills of the Durncrag mountains, your rangers will have no difficulty evading the enemy among the densely packed firs.

When the bandits have disappeared from view, you call a halt and allow your men to rest. In spite of the number of men you have lost, they are still eager to continue the mission.

Pick a number from the *Random Number Table*.

> If the number you have picked is *0–4*, turn to **51**.
> If it is *5–9*, turn to **120**.

212

An overwhelming stench of dampness and decay pervades the shaft. You decide to send one of your men up the ladder to make sure that it is still secure. All seems well for he soon reaches the next level and signals you all to follow. The tunnel on the upper level leads to an oval-shaped, rough-hewn chamber where a strange silky fluid coats the floor.

> If you have the Kai Discipline of Animal Kinship, turn to **41**.
> If you do not possess this skill, search for an exit from the chamber, and turn to **276**.

213

A thorough search uncovers the following items:

> Pickaxe
> Shovel
> Axe
> Torch
> Tinderbox
> Hourglass

If you wish to keep any of these items, remember to mark them on your *Action Chart*. (The Pickaxe and the Shovel each occupy the same amount of space in your Backpack as two normal Items.)

After satisfying yourself that there is nothing else of use in the boathouse, you order your men to launch the rowing boat.

Turn to **180**.

214

You can feel a current of dank, cold air against your face as you walk along the tunnel. The rock walls sparkle with a glistening ore that catches the light from your torch and reflects it in a dazzling display of colours. Fatigue and the distraction of the dancing lights, make you oblivious to the fungi in which you now stand. A cloud of pink spores is beginning to rise, clogging your mouth and nostrils and threatening to suffocate you unless you act quickly.

If you wish to run along the tunnel to avoid the spores, turn to **46**.

If you decide to go back to the chamber and take the south tunnel, turn to **117**.

215

Barraka carries the stench of death and decay about him. He strides into the temple, his boots of Gourgaz hide covering both legs and feet, and slams shut the huge stone door with frightening ease. He stands in silence before pushing open the huge black doors engraved with the menacing skulls. Suddenly a gale-force wind sweeps through the temple and your ears are filled by a terrible scream. Beyond the open doors, a pier of stone juts into the abyss of Maakengorge: you are staring into the chasm of doom.

Barraka turns away from the windswept pier and walks slowly towards the altar. From a hidden scabbard he removes a twisted black dagger and holds its stiletto blade to the light. An evil blue flame runs up and down the black steel spike, flickering in the ice-cold winds of Maakengorge. The sacrifice is about to begin.

If you wish to draw your weapon and attack Barraka, turn to **296**.

If you wish to distract his attention from the altar without attacking him, turn to **119**.

216

There is little that can be done to help the injured ranger. Tentacles now engulf the rowing boat from all sides and threaten to drag you all to a watery grave.

If you wish to help the other ranger who is now being dragged from the boat by his foot, turn to **304**.

If you wish to grab the oars and row for the other
side of the river, turn to **189**.

217

Your men cheer with delight at your victory and drop
through the stable roof to join you. A hard battle
follows but the bandits are soon cleared from the
stables and chased away into the stormy night.

Turn to **345**.

218

The arrow flies straight and true towards the bandit,
striking home beneath his raised arm. He screams
and falls backwards, impaling himself on his own
javelin as he crashes to the ground. You are about to
draw another arrow when you see a menacing black
shape dart across the sky; it plummets downwards
and lands on the watchtower roof. You discard your
bow and unsheathe your weapon as you race up the
stairs to investigate.

Turn to **223**.

219

It takes half an hour for you to recover from your
ordeal and to take in your new surroundings. You are
standing at the edge of a huge slag-heap, which rises
out of the dark waters of the underground river. Less
than twenty feet from the summit, a dim light
illuminates a long stone shute. You decide to take a
closer look. You soon discover that the climb is long,
slow and arduous, and only after an hour of
strenuous effort, do you finally find yourself at the top
in a small service tunnel. The tunnel is deserted

except for a mine wagon parked near to the tunnel entrance.

If you wish to examine the wagon, turn to **167**.

If you wish to ignore the wagon, begin to climb the steep tunnel by turning to **185**.

220

Your blow has unhorsed the bandit. He falls to the ground heavily, shattering his lance beneath him. He staggers to his feet and, raising the hinged eye-shield of his helm, he stares at you and smiles wickedly, exposing a jagged line of blackened teeth. He spits his battle-cry and runs towards you, unsheathing a broadsword as he closes in.

If you wish to fight the warrior, turn to **90**.

If you wish to evade combat, turn to **163**.

221

You soon reach a hall divided by a wide chasm. It is deathly quiet here and even the slightest noise seems to echo around the grey-stone walls like a clash of cymbals. An arched bridge crosses the chasm and leads to a massive pair of stone doors. You are crossing the bridge when there is a deafening rumble. The doors are opening.

If you wish to draw your weapon and prepare for combat, turn to **50**.

If you wish to flee from the bridge, run back along the tunnel and descend the stairs, by turning to **228**.

If you would rather leap from the parapet of the bridge into the unknown depths of the chasm, turn to **342**.

222

In the plush candlelit interior of the caravan you find the actor, cowering beneath a blanket in the far corner. You flick the blanket aside and ask the petrified man to explain how he came to possess such a fine sword.

'I . . . I bought it in Eshnar,' he stammers, his eyes wide with fear, 'from the innkeeper of the "Pick and Shovel" tavern.' He grasps the sword by the blade and offers it to you. 'If it is your sword I have unwittingly bought, I am truly sorry. Here, please take it.'

You grip the brass hilt and examine it closely. There is no doubt: it is a Sommlending cavalry sword, but the inscription on the blade makes your heart miss a beat: 'Captain Remir D'Val – King's Guard Regiment'.

If you wish to keep this sword, mark it on your *Action Chart* as a Weapon.

Turn to **165**.

223 – *Illustration XIII (overleaf)*

Pushing open the trapdoor, you climb out on to the watchtower roof. You are greeted by a shocking sight. The bodies of Sommlending soldiers lie scattered over the floor; their armour is rent and torn and they have all suffered terrible wounds. Over the carnage hovers a monstrous bird. Its wings beat the smoke-filled air, its razor-sharp talons slashing and mutilating everything they touch. Astride the creature sits a warrior wreathed in iron and steel, the scimitar in his hand stained with Sommlending blood. He swings one leg from his gem-encrusted saddle, pauses, and then leaps down to the watchtower roof. A voice echoes in your head as the warrior closes in.

224–225

'Say your prayers, Sommlending, for your life is soon to end!'

If you wish to fight the warrior, turn to **77**.
If you wish to evade combat, turn to **128**.

224

You can hear the harsh breath of the guards close behind you. Suddenly, the tunnel narrows and divides in two.

If you wish to enter the left tunnel, turn to **199**.
If you wish to enter the right tunnel, turn to **208**.
If you possess either the Kai Discipline of Tracking or Sixth Sense, turn to **60**.

225

You try to ignore your aching legs and the fear that knots your stomach by forcing your concentration on the sun-flag, a fluttering symbol of hope in the distance. Your face is streaked with sweat and your lungs feel as though they will burst but you dare not slacken your pace; the thought of Warhound fangs closing and tugging on your skin is all you need to drive you forward.

At four hundred yards, you can see that the barricade and watchtower are inhabited, but at this distance the faces you can see are only a line of small pink dots on the walls. At three hundred yards, you run into some gruesome remains, where the corpses of bandits lie twisted on the ground, most killed by arrows. Many have lain in the open for weeks; a flock of startled carrion crows rise shrieking from their feast as you race through the bodies. You turn away in disgust.

XIII.　Astride the creature sits a warrior wreathed in iron and steel

Suddenly a new sound drifts across the plain: the sound of cheering. The beleaguered defenders have spotted you and recognized your green Kai cloak. Two hundred yards to go. You have just passed the ruins of a burnt-out cottage when you feel an agonizing pain tear through your left thigh. An arrow has pierced your leg and you pitch forward into the mud and ash.

Crouched in the ruined cottage, a bandit sniper raises his bow and takes careful aim at your head.

Pick a number from the *Random Number Table*.

If the number you have picked is *1–5*, turn to **20**.
If it is *6–9*, turn to **300**.
If it is *0*, turn to **181**.

226

The Ruanon forest is a tangle of pale grey tree-trunks of every shape and size. Passage through these densely packed, mist-enshrouded trees is painfully slow on horseback, and you are soon forced to dismount and lead your horse by the reins.

If you wish to continue making slow progress through the forest, turn to **21**.
If you decide to forsake the forest and press on along the highway instead, turn to **82**.

227

You identify the birds as carrion crows, a despicable breed of Wildland scavengers. Whenever a creature lies dead in the wastelands you can be sure to find a host of these loathsome predators.

If you decide to take a closer look at what they are eating, turn to **328**.

If you would rather ignore them and continue your ride, turn to **120**.

228

The stairs lead directly to a lower level of the mines where a tunnel leads off to the south. You have followed this new route for nearly a mile when you arrive in a large hall. Several huge casks line the west wall, and at the far end you can see a door set into the arch of a wide staircase.

If you wish to enter the hall and advance towards the door, turn to **23**.
If you wish to make for the stairs, turn to **105**.

229

You drag the bodies into the thorny briars and conceal them before entering the crypt door. Once inside, you close the door behind you and follow a wide torchlit corridor towards the east.

Turn to **235**.

230

You make a search of the bodies and find:

> Sword
> Dagger
> 9 Gold Crowns
> Enough food for 2 Meals

You may take any of these items but be sure to mark them on your *Action Chart*.

Muffled footsteps make you glance nervously along the tunnel. Two guards are trying to creep up on you under cover of the shadows, but you turn and run before they can attack.

Turn to **224**.

231

Your attack is swift and deadly. The guard expires before his head hits the ground. A search of his clothing reveals:

> 3 Gold Crowns
> Sword
> Enough food for 1 Meal

You may take whatever you wish before you cross the bridge but remember to make the necessary adjustments to your *Action Chart*. As you reach the far side, you hear the sound of running footsteps in the distance. You decide not to wait to see who it is and quickly enter the tunnel in the west wall.

Turn to **348**.

232

You follow the river back towards the Ruanon bridge, taking care to stay hidden from the bandit horsemen who now stand guard on the bridge itself. A few

hundred yards beyond, you find a narrow track leading to a ramshackle boathouse. If it contains a boat,
you should be able to cross the river quite easily.

If you wish to investigate the boathouse, turn to **68**.
If you wish to continue downstream and look for
some other way to cross the river, turn to **130**.

233

Your rest is disturbed by the anxious shout of the
night guard: 'Awake! Awake! We're under attack!'

Throwing back their blankets, your men leap to their
feet, peering through the teeming rain at the shadowy
silhouette of horsemen circling the ruins. Suddenly
an arrow whistles through the darkness. Your look-
out screams and falls to his knees. 'Form a circle,' you
shout. 'Keep behind cover!'

The rangers gather swords and shields and press
themselves against the wet temple marble for protection. The sound of metal-shod boots on stone makes
you spin around. A dozen warriors, dressed in shiny
red armour are clambering across the broken pillars.
Two rangers run to block their advance but they are
felled by one sweep of the warrior leader's broadsword. Then the warrior sees you and quickens his
pace. His bloodied sword is raised to strike again.
You cannot evade combat and must fight the warrior
to the death.

Bandit Warrior: COMBAT SKILL 17   ENDURANCE 26

If you win, turn to **312**.

234

You barely have time to catch a breath before a
tentacle coils around your legs and drags you down.

Pick a number from the *Random Number Table*, and note this number down in the margin of your *Action Chart*. (In this instance, 0 = 10.) This number represents the number of combat rounds you can survive underwater before you begin to lose ENDURANCE points due to lack of oxygen. If you have the Kai Discipline of Mind Over Matter, you can add 2 to the number you have picked.

Giant Meresquid: COMBAT SKILL 16   ENDURANCE 37

Fight this combat as normal. If it lasts longer than the number of rounds that you can endure safely underwater, you must deduct an additional 2 ENDURANCE points for every round thereafter, due to lack of oxygen.

If you win the combat, turn to **32**.

235

The corridor ends at a flight of steps that descends a hundred feet into the earth. At the bottom, a short passage leads to a junction where a tunnel runs from north to south. To the north you can see a torchlit cavern with what appear to be observation slits carved into the wall; to the south a passage leads towards a low balcony.

If you wish to investigate the torchlit cavern, turn to **177**.

If you wish to take a look over the low balcony, turn to **100**.

236

You are approaching a large outbuilding when you hear a muffled voice. Suddenly the door bursts open to reveal two bandit warriors, their bows raised; arrows fly and rangers fall from their horses. Drawing your weapon you charge your attackers, but the other bandits appear from every side and your men are caught in a murderous crossfire.

However, the speed of your attack panics the bowmen. They turn to run but you cut them down before they have taken a few steps. Then a dark-skinned warrior with black oily hair appears at a window opposite. He flicks his hand and a knife thuds into your arm. You lose 4 ENDURANCE points. Gritting your teeth, you wrench the blade free and hurl it back. The bandit dies instantly. Clutching your wounded arm, you stagger through the building and escape through a rear door. The land that faces you now is steep and heavily forested.

If you wish to run straight into the forest, turn to **123**.

If you want to change direction as soon as you are hidden from sight, turn to **169**.

237

The bodies of your enemies lie entwined at your feet. You jump down from the parapet and run towards the open stone door, anxious to leave the bridge before the carnage is discovered. Beyond the doors, a ramp gently descends towards a tunnel in the west wall.

Turn to **348**.

238

Placing your hands on the injured man's chest, you use your healing powers to numb the pain before withdrawing the arrow. He is a lucky man; the arrow has not pierced any internal organs. Your Kai skill repairs the punctured flesh in seconds, and you help the man to his feet. With a look of open-mouthed amazement, he watches as you turn and ascend the stone steps to the watchtower roof.

Turn to **223**.

239

'They're no ordinary bandits, they're a private army. Their leader is a renegade noble from Vassagonia called Barraka, though his men call him "Doomslayer". After the first raid we thought he and his men would leave us alone – after all, this is a poor province even when the road carries traffic from the mines of Ruanon and Eshnar. But "Doomslayer" and his men have stayed. It's . . . it's as if they are determined to kill us at all costs.'

That night, the tavern-keeper's sons agree to take it in turns to sit watch at the arrow-slits, so that you and your men can get some sleep.

Turn to **324**.

240

For over ten miles, the river wends its steady course southwards. You pass through several grottos, but their rocky banks are so steep that they make a landing impossible. You are rowing along a particularly wide tunnel when you suddenly realize that the boat is moving faster and faster, and the faint sound of rushing water is gradually increasing. Soon the whole tunnel is filled with a thundering cacophony of noise.

You brace yourself in preparation for rough water, but you are totally unprepared for the sight that befalls you. Less than fifty feet away, the river disappears over the edge of a massive waterfall. Desperately your men row against the current towards the tunnel wall, but it is too late: you are caught in the current and are hurtling towards the edge of the waterfall.

Pick a number from the *Random Number Table*.

If the number that you have picked is *0–4*, turn to **94**.
If it is *5–9*, turn to **158**.

241

The ceiling of the cavern is so low that you are forced to all press yourselves against the bottom of the boat to avoid head injuries. For nearly an hour the boat is swept through a maze of underground waterways before coming to a sudden halt; you are grounded upon a bank of shingle. You are in a section of the tunnel that is much higher than any you have previously travelled. To the south the river continues into the rockface, but to the east you notice another shingle bank and a land tunnel beyond.

If you wish to row across to the other bank, abandon the boat and continue on foot, turn to **309**.
If you wish to continue by river, turn to **115**.

242

You roll aside to avoid the deadly disc but your reactions are not quick enough to save you. The razor-sharp weapon slices into your throat, knocking you backwards with the force of impact.

Your life and your mission end here.

243

D'Val runs past the wagon, leading a dozen of his best swordsmen in a counter-charge, and driving the enemy all the way back to the barricade. None escape alive. Those who survive D'Val's swordsmen are cut down on the plain by his archers as they run towards the ruins. The shout of victory has barely died away before you are faced by a new threat.

Turn to **124**.

244

You slip past the guards and enter the tunnel unseen. It is wide and illuminated by a line of wall torches, whose guttering flames crackle and splutter noisily. You soon arrive at a junction where the tunnel narrows and divides in two.

If you have the Kai Discipline of Sixth Sense or Tracking, turn to **250**.

If you do not possess either of these skills, you may enter the left tunnel by turning to **335**.

Or, if you wish, you may enter the right tunnel by turning to **11**.

245

Two well-aimed blows are enough to despatch the hissing Elix. The ranger has collapsed and is nearly unconscious through loss of blood. His right foot is almost severed at the ankle; you know that he has only a few minutes to live and there is nothing that you can do to help him. Your other man is also now beyond all help.

> If you wish to escape from the chamber by ascending the stairs, turn to **346**.
>
> If you wish to leave by descending the stairs, turn to **83**.

246

Taking great care to feel the floor ahead of you with your weapon, you advance very slowly into the dark, unaware of the eyes that are watching your every move. Hidden in the gloom are the dull satanic orbs of a Daemonak: a macabre and ghoulish vampire. Its attack is swift and silent, painless yet deadly. Before you realize that the parasite has attached itself to your back, you have lost 8 ENDURANCE points.

> If you are still alive and you possess the Sommerswerd, turn to **34**.
>
> If you are still alive but do not possess this Special Item, turn to **85**.

247

Your men look disappointed by your decision, but you are their commanding officer and they are elite soldiers of Sommerlund; they neither argue nor grumble as they follow you southward. Darkness soon engulfs the highway and you are forced to stop and set up camp by the roadside. The men gather firewood and a guard is posted on the horses. You are hungry and must now eat a Meal or lose 3 ENDURANCE points.

The night passes without incident and at dawn you break camp and continue along 'Raider's Road'.

Pick a number from the *Random Number Table*.

If the number that you have picked is *0–4*, turn to **171**.
If it is *5–9*, turn to **25**.

248

You glance over your shoulder to see a horde of warriors silhouetted in the light of the tunnel entrance. Their blood-curdling war-cries echo along the damp and gloomy shaft.

You soon reach a section where the tunnel has collapsed and a large mound of earth rises almost to the ceiling. Desperately, you climb the mound and claw your way through the narrow gap, then drop to the passageway beyond. Here you discover a loose timber prop. When everyone is clear, you barge it with your shoulder; the prop splinters and tons of earth and stone come crashing down to seal the tunnel. As the dust settles, you stare into the darkness ahead. On the walls you can just make out a line of torches. Your men gather these and light them before you continue on your way.

Turn to **254**.

249 – *Illustration XIV*

You run half-crouched to the barricade and prise a bow from the hand of a dead soldier. You have spotted the leader of the bandit cavalry; a tall dark-skinned warrior with a thin chiselled nose, rallying his horsemen at the foot of the stone watchtower. You know you must kill him before he can regroup his

XIV.   You have spotted the leader of the bandit cavalry

troops, or D'Val and his hard-pressed men will be ridden down and mercilessly slaughtered.

You notch an arrow and draw back the bowstring. The straining cord bites into your fingers as you take aim.

Pick a number from the *Random Number Table*.

If you have the Kai Discipline of Weaponskill (any weapon), add 2 to the number you have picked.

If your total is now *0–3*, turn to **153**.
If it is *4–7*, turn to **323**.
If it is *8–11*, turn to **39**.

250

You notice that the right tunnel is newly excavated, and you sense that it has yet to be completed. Rather than get caught in a dead end, you push on along the left tunnel.

Turn to **335**.

251

You are helped tonight by a cloudless sky, for the highway is illuminated by the pale moonlight. You order three of your men to scout ahead, for you know the notorious reputation this forested highway has for sudden bandit ambushes; the densely packed trees lining the road could easily conceal an army of robbers. Before the scouts gallop away, you order them to report anything unusual they may find on the road ahead.

Within an hour, you arrive at a junction where a track from the east meets the main highway. Abandoned at the side of the road is a burnt-out wagon. You sense that something is wrong; your scouts should have reported this wagon long before you found it, and your men are worried by what may have happened to them. You know that you dare not continue your ride in case you fall into an ambush. You decide to rest at the junction and wait for the return of your scouts. Six hours later, as the sun slowly rises over the eastern treeline, your scouts have still not returned.

If you wish to search the highway ahead, turn to **175**.

If you wish to examine the burnt-out wagon, turn to **38**.

If you wish to explore the eastern track, turn to **293**.

252

You lead your men in single file into the forest, but in less than a minute, the trees have become far too dense for you to be able to continue on horseback. You are forced to dismount and hide your horses before continuing on foot. Then, by a great stroke of luck, you find a narrow track leading to a ramshackle boathouse at the edge of the River Xane. If it contains a boat, you should be able to cross the river with ease.

If you wish to investigate the boathouse, turn to **68**.

If you wish to continue downstream and look for some other way of crossing the river, turn to **130**.

253

You are about to order your men to make camp when a scout gallops towards you from the east. He points to a line of horsemen on the horizon. 'Bandits!' he cries. You estimate that there are at least two hundred of them and they are riding in your direction.

If you have reached the Kai rank of Warmarn (you possess 8 Kai Disciplines), turn to **72**.

If you have yet to reach this level of training, turn to **135**.

254

The tunnel continues to descend for several hundred yards until you reach a wide chamber with a timber floor. Two pairs of footprints can clearly be seen in the silt covering the rotten planks; to your horror, they both seem to disappear into a gaping hole.

Inching your way to the jagged edge, you can make out two bodies lying at the bottom of a muddy shaft. You have found your scouts but they are beyond all help. As the soft timbers begin to sag, you retreat from the edge to avoid a similar fate. Beyond the hole are two exits from this chamber. One passage heads towards the east, the other south.

If you have the Kai Discipline of Tracking, turn to **326**.

If you do not possess this skill, you may enter the east tunnel by turning to **156**.

Alternatively you can enter the south tunnel by turning to **101**.

255

You must rally the defenders or all is lost. You order two soldiers to help the Captain, and then leap on an overturned wagon in order to see clearly the enemy advance. They have already reached the ruined perimeter of Ruanon, and are now creeping forward under cover of the broken cottage walls. You shout orders to D'Val's men to defend the barricade, but the enemy are less than one hundred yards from the wall; you are afraid it might be too late to repel their attack.

Turn to **186**.

256

You slip many times on the rickety bridge, but eventually make your way across to the other side. You can just make out the jagged tunnel wall by the faint light cast by a swarm of mine flies. You press onwards, but you are now so tired that you are soon forced to stop and sleep.

Many hours pass before you awake and continue your exploration.

Turn to **309**.

257

The door is unlocked and opens into a small room with a straw-covered floor. A large iron-belted chest

rests at the foot of an unmade bed, beyond which lies another door.

If you wish to examine the chest, turn to **302**.

If you wish to ignore it and investigate the door, turn to **131**.

258 – *Illustration XV*

You quickly leave the hut far behind and press on through the trees. By morning, you have reached the edge of the forest. Staring out across the fields of tall crops you see a small village lying at the base of a shallow valley. The fields are only separated by narrow tracks, which are alive with flying insects hovering in swarms.

You are walking along the track when you suddenly spot bandits ahead. They are wandering idly up the track towards you, their spears slung over their shoulders.

If you possess an Onyx Medallion, turn to **305**.

If you wish to dive into the tall crops and hide, turn to **159**.

If you have the Kai Discipline of Camouflage *and* you have reached the Kai Rank of Guardian or higher, turn to **49**.

259

'Go away!' shouts a nervous voice. 'We're a tavern, not a barracks!' shouts another. You try to reason with them but they are adamant; they will not let you enter. You have no choice but to continue along the highway.

Turn to **141**.

XV.   The bandits are wandering idly up the track towards you

260

The Warhounds spread out and stream towards the barricade, their eyes aflame with evil intent. A group of five snarling dogs tear through the wall of sacks and casks and engulf the soldiers around you. Lashing out, you despatch two of the loathsome dogs with one swipe, but in the heat of battle you fail to notice the Warhounds that are diving towards your back. They pitch you forward into the collapsed barricade; before you can free yourself, they have sunk their fangs into your legs.

Vassagonian Warhounds:
COMBAT SKILL 18   ENDURANCE 30

If you are still alive after 3 rounds of combat, turn to **311**.

261

On the first body that you search you find:

8 Gold Crowns
Enough food for 1 Meal

You are about to search the others when you hear the sound of running footsteps approaching from the other side of the chamber. You pull the rope once more and breathe a sigh of relief as the portcullis rises into the ceiling. Rolling under the widening gap, you jump to your feet and make a hasty escape along the tunnel.

Turn to **348**.

262

You leap forward to strike but the bandit rears his steed to avert your attack. You feel the horse's flailing hooves crash down on your head and you are quickly trampled into the blood-soaked ground. Concussed and mortally wounded, the last thing that you remember of this world is the evil sneer of the bandit horseman as he raises his longsword for the death-blow.

Your life and your mission end here.

263

You twist to one side to avoid it, but the disc bites deeply into your shoulder. You lose 4 ENDURANCE points. Clutching your wounded arm, you sprint along a narrow alleyway that leads to a mass of densely packed firs. As you reach the trees you hear the shouts of bandits close behind.

> If you wish to press on through the trees towards the south, turn to **123**.
> If you wish to change direction and head west, turn to **169**.

264

Your Kai sense enables you to identify the hoof prints disappearing along the path towards the east as those made by a Sommlending cavalry horse.

> If you wish to follow the prints, turn to **134**.
> If you wish to head in the opposite direction to the tracks, turn to **191**.

265

There is no time to search the bodies. Other patrols have been alerted by the struggle and are now hacking their way through the trees to reach you. Parting the blood-stained foliage, you leap from the trees and run for Ruanon.

Turn to **307**.

'We've heard nothing for nearly a month,' he says, shaking his bearded face from side to side. 'Some horsemen from your country passed here about that time, but since then all we have seen are a travelling band of troubadours from Cloeasia and those accursed bandits.'

The tavern-keeper's sons each take it in turn to sit watch at the arrow-slits, so that you and your men can get some sleep.

Turn to **324**.

267

A terrible pain racks your chest as you are thrown backwards by the force of the crossbow bolt. You claw at the unyielding shaft, catching a glimpse of the face of an enemy guard as he raises his sword to deliver the coup de grace.

Your life and your mission end here.

268

A thorough search of the two guards reveals the following items:

> 4 Gold Crowns
> Spear
> Broadsword
> Iron Key
> Brass Key
> Enough food for 2 Meals
> Potion of Red Liquid

You recognize the liquid to be Laumspur, a potion of healing. If swallowed after combat, it will restore 4 ENDURANCE points. You may take any of the above items but be sure to mark them on your *Action Chart*.

Set into the north wall of the well chamber is a large iron door. Next to the door, a stone archway leads to a spiral staircase.

If you wish to examine the iron door, turn to **118**.
If you wish to ascend the spiral stairs, turn to **170**.
If you wish to descend the spiral stairs, turn to **228**.

269

You follow the passage for nearly an hour before finding yourself in front of a solid rockface. Shovels and barrows lie discarded upon the floor as if the excavation was abandoned in a great hurry. You may take one of the Shovels if you wish, but it will occupy the same space in your Backpack as two normal items.

You are now hungry and you must eat a Meal or lose 3 ENDURANCE points. Cursing your bad luck, you are forced to retrace your steps all the way back to the junction.

Continue your exploration by turning to **145**.

270

The rain and the gloom hide your approach and you reach the marble stairs unseen. The steps are overgrown with mould and weeds, but a path has been trod through them leading into the darkness of a huge underground vault.

If you possess a Torch in your Backpack, turn to **29**.

If you possess a Firesphere, turn to **168**.

If you have neither of these items, you can continue your way forward in darkness, and turn to **246**.

Alternatively, you can leave the vault and attempt to enter the temple via the crypt door by turning to **183**.

271

You are halfway across the bridge when someone pulls the hanging rope. You glance back, and to your horror you see that the rope travels through a series of metal rings that lead to a couple of locking pins anchoring the bridge floor to the edge of the shaft. A shiver runs down your spine as the rope snaps taut and the pegs rise out of the floor.

Pick a number from the *Random Number Table*.

If you possess the Kai Discipline of Hunting, add 2 to the number you have picked.

If your total is now *0–6*, turn to **9**.
If it is *7–11*, turn to **104**.

272

You smash feet first into a large river boulder. Recoiling from the impact, you cough uncontrollably in your desperate fight for air as the water fills your ears and nose. Down and down, around and around you go, your eyes stinging and the pain in your legs grinding agonizingly upwards through your body. A glancing blow to your shoulder rips the sleeve from your jacket and numbs your arm; your weapon falls from your hand. You are sommersaulted into a steep V-shaped channel and buffeted on all sides as you tumble towards a pool far below. You feel the sheer weight and volume of water behind you will plunge you to your doom, and as you plummet into the swirling dark water, all consciousness rapidly gives way to a blind and silent numbness.

When you open your eyes it is dusk. You have been washed up on the river bank near to a twisting forest track. The silhouette of the Maaken range rises steeply to the east, and you realize that you must have drifted many miles downstream. You have survived a terrible ordeal; one that would have killed any lesser mortal. You have lost 5 ENDURANCE points due to leg and head wounds, and one Weapon. All of your Special Items, Backpack Items and Gold Crowns are still intact. Make all the necessary adjustments to your *Action Chart* before turning to **79**.

273 – *Illustration XVI*

You have ridden less than five miles when you see a group of wagons on the highway ahead. They are painted in a gaudy mix of bright colours and drawn by teams of oxen. A huge tasselled banner flies above the leading wagon, which bears the following proclamation:

The Famous Asajir Players – Troubadours to the Imperial Courts of Magnamund

If you wish to stop to question these travelling minstrels, turn to **37**.

If you wish to ignore them and let them pass, turn to **126**.

274

Barraka draws a razor-sharp scimitar, holding its mirror-like blade in his other hand. He advances towards you with deadly grace; you can sense his warrior prowess, his ice-cold nerve. Your fight will be hard and to the death.

If you possess a Flask of Holy Water, turn to **283**.

If you do not possess this Special Item, turn to **325**.

275

With one slice of your golden sword, the timber splinters in two. A shudder runs through the ground and with one mighty roar, a deluge of earth and stone completely fills the tunnel. Clouds of dust engulf you and the force of the blast throws you to the floor; all the torches are extinguished. You lose 1 ENDURANCE point. Staggering to your feet, you hurry along the dust-choked tunnel to where the wall torches are still burning.

Turn to **335**.

XVI.   You see a group of wagons on the highway ahead

276

A hideous groan reverberates through the chamber making everyone freeze in mid-step. With mounting horror, you watch as the far wall suddenly moves towards you. A crack appears, widening to reveal a row of razor-sharp teeth. You have awoken a hungry Stoneworm and it intends to feast on your flesh. Your men unsheathe their swords and prepare for combat; it is too late for them to turn and run.

If you wish to stand and fight the Stoneworm, turn to **88**.

If you wish to escape from the chamber, you run back to the ladder and turn to **26**.

277

You kick the dead Warhound away and steel yourself for another onslaught. Three more of the snarling beasts are ready to pounce and you must fight them as one enemy.

Vassagonian Warhounds:
COMBAT SKILL 22   ENDURANCE 35

If you win the combat, turn to **155**.

278

Your lightning reactions have saved you from certain death. The deadly disc whistles past, embedding itself deep in a wheel. Rolling clear of the wagon, you sprint along a narrow alleyway leading to a knot of densely packed firs. You reach the trees but as you dive for cover, you hear the shouts of bandits close behind.

If you wish to press on through the trees towards the south, turn to **123**.

If you wish to change direction and head west, turn to **169**.

279

As you unfurl the Scroll and begin to read its ominous contents, the Baron struggles to his feet. Word for word he echoes the prophetic verse.

> When the full moon shines o'er the temple deep,
> A sacrifice will stir from sleep
> The legions of a long forgotten lord.
> When a fair royal maid on the altar dies,
> The dead of Maakengorge shall rise
> To claim their long-awaited reward.

'You must save her, Lone Wolf. You must prevent the sacrifice.' The Baron's voice is choked with emotion.

'Save who? Who must he save?' questions Captain D'Val, as he tries to calm the distressed Baron.

'My daughter, Madelon. Barraka has found the Dagger of Vashna. He plans to sacrifice my daughter upon the altar of Maaken to release the undead of Maakengorge.'

The Baron explains that during the Age of the Black Moon, King Ulnar of Sommerlund killed the mightiest of all the Darklords, Vashna, with the Sommerswerd, the sword of the sun. His body and the bodies of all his soldiers were hurled into the bottomless abyss of Maakengorge. 'He plans to lead the dead to victory; first to conquer Sommerlund and then all of the Lastlands,' he says in despair.

You stare at the Baron in stunned silence. If Barraka

280

completes the sacrifice, all is lost. What mortal army can stand against a legion of the dead?

Captain D'Val ushers you from the chamber and closes the door. 'I feared he was insane, but your Scroll confirms my worst nightmare. He speaks the truth!'

As the dreadful significance of the verse begins to sink in, your thoughts are broken by the shrill blast of a war-horn. Captain D'Val strides over to an arrow-slit and peers out across the plain. As he turns to speak, you notice his face is ashen grey. 'The bandits . . . they're launching an attack!'

If you possess Captain D'Val's sword, turn to **327**.
If you do not possess it, turn to **289**.

280

You roll the body over on to its side and make a quick search. You discover:

> 3 Gold Crowns
> Enough food for 1 Meal
> Sword

You may take whatever you wish before crossing the bridge but remember to make the necessary adustments to your *Action Chart*. Upon reaching the far side, you detect the sound of running footsteps somewhere in the distance. You decide against waiting to see who it is, and leave the chamber by a tunnel in the west wall.

Turn to **348**.

281

The creature vanishes and you find yourself lying on the tunnel floor. You are breathless, your heart is pounding and your skin feels cold and damp. You begin to realize what must have happened to you. The fungi spores were making you hallucinate; the Tunnel Fiend existed only in your mind, it was nothing more than an illusion. Unfortunately, any ENDURANCE points you lost in combat with this mere illusion cannot be restored: you inflicted the wounds on yourself, striking your body against the jagged tunnel walls.

As the effects of the spores begin to fade, you are overwhelmed by fatigue and lose consciousness. Many hours pass before you awake to a painfully sore throat and aching head. You re-light your torch and push on along the tunnel.

Turn to **185**.

282

The lock is rusty and stiff but eventually it gives and the door opens. You enter a narrow passageway that descends to another door fifty feet away. You order your men to go on ahead while you secure the door. It takes a great effort to force the lock closed. You hear the hollow click of the lock, but this is echoed by a click far louder. A trap has been sprung. The floor opens in the centre of the passage and swallows all your men, screaming with terror into the void below. With fear rising in your throat, you race to the edge and peer into the inky black pit. The walls are sheer and its depth unknown. A cold breeze on your face and the eerie sound of wind whistling through the chasm is all that meets your desperate stare. With heavy heart, you bid a silent farewell to your lost men and hurry towards the distant door.

Turn to **257**.

283

You grasp the Flask, take careful aim, and hurl it straight and true. Barraka stares open-mouthed as the container shatters against the black steel dagger. There is an explosion of searing white flame. The heat scorches your face and you are thrown to the floor. You lose 3 ENDURANCE points.

You stare in horror as Barraka, his arm torn from his body by the blast, staggers backwards across the temple. He has been blinded by the fire and he claws at his sightless eyes with his remaining hand. You watch in silence as he stumbles through the black skull doors and plummets into Maakengorge, swallowed up by the chasm of doom.

Turn to **350**.

284

You order your men to form a line and advance towards the oncoming bandits. They are less than a hundred yards away when you give the order to charge. The wind whips your face, carrying the echo of battle-cries across the plain as you close on the enemy. As your forces clash, you are stunned by the shock of impact. Your horse collides with the flank of a bandit steed, hurling it and its rider to the ground. You reel in the saddle and are unable to avoid a spear thrust that opens a wound in your thigh. You lose 3 ENDURANCE points before turning to face your attacker.

Bandit Warrior: COMBAT SKILL 16   ENDURANCE 25

You can evade combat at any time by turning to **89**.
If you win the combat, turn to **7**.

285

You storm the steps and attack. The guards fire a volley of deadly bolts and a metal-tipped shaft passes straight through the hood of your cloak. Miraculously, you are unharmed. You raise your weapon and strike, cracking the neck of the guard who fired at you. No sooner has he fallen than another steps forward to take his place. There is no room to evade combat and you must fight him to the death.

Guard: COMBAT SKILL 16   ENDURANCE 28

If you win the combat, turn to **71**.

286

You wait with bated breath as a line of haggard men file past your barely concealed hiding place. An escort of bandit warriors urge them forward, beating any who falter or step out of the line. Then each man is forced to take hold of a wagon and push it back along the tunnel. Soon they have all disappeared from view.

You wait, and when you are sure that the coast is clear you step back into the tunnel and press on, taking care to keep well in the shadows. You finally reach a point where the tunnel emerges into daylight. To your left, a dense copse has been cut back from the entrance, and wagon tracks lead to a timber gantry above a mound of ore. The men and the guards who passed you are now at the gantry, but they fail to see you sprint from the entrance and dive into the trees. A brief pause for breath is all you allow yourself before setting off through the trees towards Ruanon.

Turn to **200**.

287

You have barely taken a dozen steps when the old woman drops to the floor. A ranger shouts 'Ambush!' It is the last word he will ever speak. A razor-sharp disc of metal whistles down from the balcony above and sinks into his chest. Then, suddenly, the tavern is full of bandits, pouring in through windows and doors. Three charge straight at you, their battle-cries loud and savage. You draw your weapon and strike, beheading two of the dark-skinned warriors with a single blow. The third bandit is upon you before the bodies of the others have fallen to the floor.

Bandit Warrior: COMBAT SKILL 17   ENDURANCE 27

If you win the fight, turn to **75**.

288

You leave three men to guard the horses and take four men into the mine. It is pitch dark but you are quick to notice that unlit torches line the damp walls at regular intervals. You each take a torch and light it before going any further. Now the footprints can clearly be seen on the muddy floor. They lead to a collapsed section of the tunnel where they disappear over the top of a massive earthfall.

> If you wish to climb the mound of earth and squeeze through the narrow gap between the top of the mound and the ceiling, turn to **254**.
> If you decide to call off the search and return to the mine entrance, turn to **187**.

289 – *Illustration XVII (overleaf)*

You follow Captain D'Val as he hurries down the broad watchtower steps and out to the barricade. A rolling sound like distant thunder fills the air. Cavalry are pouring on to the plain from all sides, grouping up into battalions in preparation for the advance. Columns of foot soldiers in bright scarlet armour march through their ranks, herding a frightened wall of people before them.

'They're Ruanese!' cries D'Val, his hand shielding the light from his eyes. 'That cur Barraka; he's using them as a shield!'

All around you, the Captain's men have drawn their bowstrings, awaiting his signal to fire. But it is an order he dare not give. Suddenly a hidden catapult hurls a massive black rock through the air, straight towards the barricade. You stare in horror as it bursts into flame and disintegrates, showering a rain of blazing oil on everyone beneath. The soldiers cannot evade the deluge and many are badly burnt before the flames are

XVII.   You stare in horror as a deluge of blazing oil rains down

smothered. A battle-cry resounds from the enemy ranks: the signal to attack. The Ruanese are pushed aside and trampled by the onrush of scarlet warriors who now race towards the barricade.

The blazing oil has scattered D'Val's men, and the barricade is poorly defended. You hear D'Val shout your name. His cloak and tunic are ablaze and he is screaming for your help.

If you wish to help the Captain, turn to **5**.

If you wish to rally the defenders before the enemy reach the barricade, turn to **86**.

If you have reached the Kai rank of Warmarn (you possess 8 Kai Disciplines), turn to **255**.

290

The ruins are overgrown with weeds and roots, but you can make out the shape of the inner sanctum of the temple quite distinctly. The huge marble canopy is still intact and will serve as an excellent shelter from the storm. As you tie your horse to a withered shrub, you glance up to see two men hiding beneath the

canopy, dressed in long black robes. You order them to come out and identify themselves, but they neither move nor answer your call.

If you wish to signal your men to attack the robed strangers, turn to **44**.

If you wish to try to capture them alive, turn to **102**.

If you decide to sheathe your weapon and approach them, your hand extended in a gesture of friendship, turn to **78**.

291

The passage leads to an iron-studded door. Placing your ear to the rough wood, you detect the sound of voices.

If you have the Kai Discipline of Camouflage, turn to **172**.

If you do not possess this skill, you can draw your weapon, open the door, and turn to **93**.

Alternatively you can retrace your steps back to the gallery and take the other exit by turning to **55**.

292

You draw the sword just in time to save yourself. The deadly disc is sliced in two on the edge of your golden blade and the semi-circles of twisted steel scream past barely inches from your cheeks. You roll away from the wagon and sprint along a narrow alleyway leading to a bank of dense trees. As you enter the trees, you hear the shouts of the bandits close behind.

If you wish to press on towards the south, turn to **123**.

If you want to change direction and head west, turn to **169**.

293

You follow the track as it wends its way through the forested hills. You soon come across fresh hoof prints in the soft earth of the track.

If you have the Kai Discipline of Tracking, turn to **18**.

If you do not possess this skill, turn to **150**.

294

The wagon halts in the centre of the timber gantry and the men are herded back into the tunnel. You wait for over an hour before the entrance is free of guards, then you slip out of the wagon and run back along the gantry. A copse of densely packed trees lines one side of the track and along the other is a sheer drop into the quarry. As you dash into the foliage, you suddenly realize that the whispering stranger had been trying to help you escape. You bid him silent thanks and press on towards Ruanon.

Turn to **200**.

295

The bandit warrior lies dead at your feet. 'For Sommerlund!' you cry, as the enemy shield-wall falters and falls. Your men take up the battle-cry and hurl themselves against the foe. Swords whine and men and metal cry out in pain. The fight is desperate but swift. The bandits throw down their shields and flee the tavern, melting away into the rain-filled darkness. You rally your troops and run to the stables, but your heart sinks when you see the doors are wide open. You fear the worst.

Turn to **345**.

296

If you possess the Sommerswerd, turn to **122**.
If you have a Flask of Holy Water, turn to **283**.
If you do not possess either, turn to **274**.

297

It is noon before you are forced to call a halt. You have reached the edge of a ridge where the highway begins a long descent towards a wide wooden bridge. This is the Ruanon bridge: you recognize its stout black timbers and the dark waters of the River Xane that flow beneath. On the far side of the bridge lie the fire-blackened ruins of an inn and the unmistakable silhouette of bandit horsemen. At the entrance to the bridge is a white signpost pointing across the bridge to the south.

RUANON – 12 MILES

You know it would be suicidal to attempt to cross the bridge: the bandit horsemen each carry a heavy crossbow slung from their saddle.

If you wish to try to cross the river further upstream to the west, turn to **113**.
If you wish to try to cross the river downstream, to the east, turn to **252**.

298

Suddenly the Tunnel Fiends that are screaming and writhing beneath your blows, fade and disappear. You shake your head in disbelief and rub your eyes, but no trace of their bodies remains. You slowly begin to realize what has happened. The fungi spores are making you hallucinate; the creatures existed only in your mind, and were nothing more than illusions.

Unfortunately, any ENDURANCE points you lost in combat are not restored – during the 'fight' you have collided many times with the jagged tunnel walls. You sheathe your weapon and stagger away from the fungi, eager to leave them far behind.

Turn to **185**.

299

Quickly you pull you men into line, shoulder to shoulder across the entrance to the mine. Their shields form a wall of wood and steel to deflect the arrows now falling from the sky. As they flood out from the trees, the bandit warriors discard their bows in favour of long, curved swords. Many of them stumble and fall but their leader beats them forward with the flat of his battle-axe. He is an ugly brute dressed in a heavy brass hauberk. As the first of the enemy smash into the shield-wall, he screams a deafening war-cry. A numbing thunder of blows rain down as the bandits hew and slice into your line. The fight is bitter but the wall holds firm, as your men bravely defend themselves.

The first wave of bandits stagger back clutching their wounds, a dozen left dead at your feet. None of your

men have fallen. However, you barely have time to wipe your blood-spattered brow before their leader bounds towards you, his battle-axe sweeping the air. He batters his way through the shield-wall and attacks you. You cannot evade him and must fight him to the death.

Bandit Leader: COMBAT SKILL 19   ENDURANCE 29

If you win the fight, turn to **121**.

300

A scream of pain and terror fills the air. The sniper crashes to the ground as the jaws of a Warhound clamp tightly around his neck. Other hounds are drawn by his ghastly screams and he is soon ripped to pieces. You look up to see a man running towards you from the barricade. He has a shield in one hand and a longbow in the other; it is Captain D'Val.

He reaches you, breathless from his run, and draws an arrow from his quiver. The Warhounds, tired of their victim, are in search of fresh sport and are turning their attentions on you. D'Val aims and fires, drawing another arrow as soon as his bow is empty. Warhounds tumble and crash to the ground around you, felled by D'Val's deadly shafts. The Captain grabs you by the arm and swings you over his shoulder in one swift movement, before carrying you back to the barricade. Others run forward to help him, but the bandit archers are now in range and the men are forced back by a hail of arrows. The red shafts whistle past on all sides. Finally you reach the barricade; a wagon is pulled aside and you are carried through the open gap. Captain D'Val is close to exhaustion; he staggers and his men rush to catch him before he drops you to the ground.

Turn to **341**.

301

The street continues past a stable with a large paddock. The enclosure is full of horses, all of which are saddled.

If you possess the Kai Discipline of Animal Kinship, turn to **106**.

If you do not posses this skill, turn to **236**.

302

The chest appears to be unlocked, but with the loss of your men still fresh in your mind, you decide to take no chances. Standing to one side, you ease open the chest with the tip of your weapon and flick back the lid. You wait with bated breath but nothing happens; whoever lives in this room must be confident that the pit trap will foil any would-be thieves, for the chest contains an assortment of loot. There are plates and goblets of gem-encrusted gold, necklaces of turquoise, pearls and statuettes of marbled jadin, a rare and precious stone. You marvel at their beauty but decide against taking them for they are heavy and of little practical use. Then you notice a soft leather bag beneath the gold plates. When you pull it out of the chest, you immediately recognize its distinctive shape. It is a herbwarden's satchel and contains the following items:

2 Potions of Laumspur – Each restores 4 ENDURANCE points

1 Potion of Alether – Increases COMBAT SKILL by
  2 points for the duration of one combat.
1 Flask of Holy Water

If you wish to keep any of these items, mark them on
your *Action Chart*.

  Examine the far door and turn to **131**.

303

Your knees and knuckles are badly bruised, but you
are still alive and clinging to the wooden bridge floor.
You lose 2 ENDURANCE points. However, the slatted
floor of the bridge makes an excellent ladder and you
waste no time in climbing out of the mine shaft. Your
enemies scream and curse at you from the other side
of the chamber, for they are now trapped there and
unable to pursue you. With a wry smile you wave
them farewell before entering a tunnel in the west
wall.

  Turn to **348**.

304

One blow is enough to sever the writhing tentacle and
free the ranger. He shouts his thanks and quickly
slices the tip from another rubbery limb as it rises from
the slime-stained river. Suddenly there is a tremendous crack as yet another tentacle punches its way
through the bottom of the boat. The boat is lifted into
the air and you are hurled into the icy cold water.

Pick a number from the *Random Number Table*.

  If the number you have picked is 0–4, turn to **47**.
  If the number is 5–9, turn to **234**.

305

A bold plan springs to mind. You remove the Onyx
Medallion from your pocket and stride boldly
towards the bandit spearmen. They are so busy talk-
ing to each other that they fail to see you. Your
appearance comes as a sudden shock. Acting your
part to perfection, you scold them for their sloven-
linesss and threaten to report them to Barraka himself. As their eyes fall upon the Onyx Medallion, you
can almost hear their hearts miss a beat. Frantically
they pull themselves together and stand to attention, awaiting your next command. You send them
marching off towards the forest and then hurry away
in the opposite direction, just in case they realize that
they have been tricked.

Turn to **204**.

306

Your men push open the door with their swords and
quickly enter. You hear a muffled voice and a ranger
soon reappears at the door. 'It is safe, my Lord,' he
says, and stands aside to allow you to enter.

Turn to **84**.

307

From all along the forest edge, groups of bandits
emerge from the trees, whipped and scolded by their
bullying sergeants for allowing you to escape. This
spurs you to quicken your pace and you cover the
first hundred yards with ease. Then arrows begin to
fall around you. You duck and weave, making yourself a difficult target for the archers, and gradually the
falling shafts dwindle in number. You smile at their

futile attempts to stop you, but your confidence is soon shaken by a pack of snarling Warhounds breaking out of the woods to your right; they are off the leash and hungry for blood. You are less than five hundred yards from Ruanon but the Warhounds are closing in.

If you wish to quicken your pace and try to outrun them, turn to **225**.

If you wish to stop and fight them, turn to **36**.

308 – *Illustration XVIII*

You turn the key and push open the iron door. Immediately, a loud hissing fills your ears, like steam escaping from a geyser. A cat-like creature leaps at you from out of the darkness knocking you to the ground, its eyes glowing with a green fire and its fetid breath scorching your face – it is an Elix! As you struggle to free yourself from its powerful fanged jaws, more of these creatures bound through the open door and attack your men. You cannot evade combat and you must fight this beast to the death.

Elix: COMBAT SKILL 17   ENDURANCE 30

If you win the combat, turn to **127**.

309

You follow the tunnel for three hours before arriving at a great hall where several tunnels, all at different depths, meet up. A series of wide stone ramps connect each tunnel to those immediately above and below. Four levels below you, teams of men are pushing wagonloads of ore. Others, dressed in red

XVIII.   A loud hissing fills your ears, like steam escaping from a geyser

310

armour, stand guard over the wagon-pushers and urge them on with whips and curses.

The tunnel in which you now stand is on the highest level. You realize that the only way you can proceed is by descending the ramp to a tunnel on a lower level. To your dismay, you notice that each of the ramps are guarded by armed men. Inching forward, you peer over the edge of the ramp; two guards are sitting near the tunnel entrance below. They are laughing and giggling and pointing at an empty wine flagon that lies at their feet. After watching them for several minutes you decide they are probably too drunk to notice you. You decide to make a dash for the tunnel.

Pick a number from the *Random Number Table*. If you possess the Kai Discipline of Camouflage, add 4 to the number you have picked.

If your total is now *0–7*, turn to **138**.
If your total is *8–13*, turn to **244**.

310

You are less than ten yards from the watchtower door when a spear-haft knocks you to the ground. You roll aside in time to avoid a deadly thrust, and spring to your feet to face your assailant. He is a hard-faced warrior with eyes as black as coal, his armour tarnished with the blood of his dead horse. He raises his spear and stabs at your chest. You cannot evade combat and must fight him to the death.

Vassagonian Warrior:
COMBAT SKILL 18   ENDURANCE 25

If you win the combat, turn to **24**.

311

Three Sommlending soldiers come to your aid. Their swords slice into the evil Warhounds until both dogs stiffen and die, and you thankfully stagger to your feet and try to assess the situation as the battle rages all around. Sommlending soldiers still man the barricade, forming in groups that hold firm where the wall does not. Spears and arrows arc through the sky piercing metal, wood and flesh. Men fall from their horses, horses scream and bolt and the dead and the wounded lie everywhere.

The Warhounds have been driven back upon the spears of their masters, who now advance behind a wall of shields. To your right, a bandit warrior is trying to jump his horse across the barricade, but the animal is wounded and near to death. It cannot make the jump; the rider is hurled forwards over the wall, falling close behind you.

If you wish to attack the bandit warrior, turn to **90**.

If you wish to rally the Sommlending soldiers to repel the advancing spearmen, turn to **3**.

312

All around you the ruins echo to the clash of weapons and the screech of battle-cries. These armour-clad horsemen are no ordinary bandit clan; they fight with a discipline and skill unheard of among the lowly outlaws of the Wildlands.

You step over the dead warrior and call about you a handful of your men. The enemy have surrounded your horses and you must act quickly if you are to save them from being taken. You lead a charge through the ruins, piercing the enemy line. They falter and flee back into the darkness. However, by the time you have reached the temple perimeter, only eleven of your horses remain – the others have vanished.

After much thought, you decide to choose ten rangers to continue the mission with you, sending the remainder of your company back to Sommerlund to report what has happened. As the gloomy light of dawn gradually fills the sky, you and your chosen companions bid a sad farewell to those who must march back on foot.

Pick a number from the *Random Number Table*.

If the number you have picked is *0–2*, turn to **120**.
If it is *3–9*, turn to **51**.

313

You lay your hands on the wounded ranger and manage to set the bones in his shattered elbow, binding them tightly with cloth strips torn from his tunic. Meanwhile, the other man has freed his ensnared leg, and severed two more of the slimy tentacles that cling to the battered hull. Then he grabs the oars and frantically rows towards the distant bank, but the blades of the oars have barely entered the water when there is a tremendous crack.

Turn to **96**.

314

The forest is patrolled by bandits, but they take little interest in their guard duties and you find it easy to avoid them in the dark. Then, by chance, you come across a small log cabin hidden deep in the woods. A candle flickers at the window and the door is ajar.

If you wish to enter the hut, turn to **53**.

If you do not wish to enter the hut, continue your mission by turning to **258**.

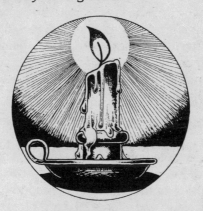

315

In the flickering light of your Torch, you can see that the tunnel is supported by a criss-cross of props and beams. The rock is damp and a narrow rivulet of ore-stained water runs along the tunnel floor. You soon reach a junction where the tunnel heads off to the left and right.

If you wish to go left, turn to **269**.

If you wish to go right, turn to **145**.

If you possess the Kai Discipline of Tracking, turn to **48**.

316

You are halfway across when one of your men slips and is washed away by the torrential river water. His desperate cries alert the bandits. Suddenly a bandit warrior appears on top of the boulder behind which you are hiding. He screams and lunges at you with his spear. Deduct 2 from your COMBAT SKILL for the duration of the fight, for you are at a disadvantage. The bandit warrior towers over you and your footing is wet and slippery.

Bandit Warrior: COMBAT SKILL 16   ENDURANCE 26

You may evade combat at any time by diving into the River Xane. Turn to **31**.

If you win the combat, turn to **146**.

317

You concentrate your powers and direct them at an outcrop of loose shale overhanging the shaft on the opposite side of the chamber. In seconds, there is a crack of slate and stone as part of the outcrop crumbles away and falls into the gaping mine shaft. The guard is startled by the sudden noise and leaves his post to investigate. Without a moment's hesitation, you dash across the now empty bridge and disappear into the tunnel beyond.

Turn to **348**.

318 – *Illustration XIX*

Oren Vanalund is the fifteenth baron of Ruanon, a noble warrior of royal lineage, and fifth in succession to the throne of Sommerlund. This once proud and chivalrous war-lord now lies upon the cold stone floor of the chamber, red-eyed and whimpering like a frightened dog. 'He has lost everything,' says D'Val quietly. 'Barraka has destroyed his castle, his land, his

XIX. 'He has lost everything . . . his castle, his land, his town and
his family . . .'

town, and his family. His sons are dead and his only daughter has been taken captive by Barraka himself. I fear the ordeal has turned his mind.'

The pathetic man raises his tear-stained face, and with feeble voice mutters a curious rhyme, over and over again.

'When a fair royal maid on the altar dies,
The dead of Maakengorge shall rise.'

If you possess a Scroll, turn to **279**.
If you do not possess a Scroll, turn to **57**.

319

The food is delicious. You eat your fill and then make preparations for a good night's sleep. At dawn, you and your company bid farewell to the travelling players and continue on your mission to Ruanon.

Pick a number from the *Random Number Table*.

If the number you have picked is *0–4*, turn to **25**.
If it is *5–9*, turn to **171**.

320

The two guards are completely unprepared for your attack. They have only just drawn their swords when your men reach them and knock them both to the ground.

'Shall we despatch them immediately, my Lord?' asks a ranger, his sword tip at the throat of a nervous guard.

'No,' you reply. 'Tie them. They may be of some use to us yet.'

If you wish to search them, turn to **268**.
If you wish to question them, turn to **76**.

321

The foul creature lets out a ghastly shriek and dies, but its huge slimy body trembles and convulses for several minutes. You wait for a while before daring to squeeze past it to the chamber beyond. No trace of your men remain. Their bodies lie partially digested inside the Stoneworm carcass. With nausea rising in your throat, you turn and flee from this terrible chamber.

Turn to **309**.

322

Extinguishing your Torch you curl up on the floor and quickly fall into a deep sleep. Many hours pass before you awake, totally refreshed by your rest. Restore 2 ENDURANCE points.

Relighting your torch, you can now see that the hut is full of mining tools. Picks, Shovels and wheelbarrows are stacked upright along the far wall.

If you wish to take either a Pick or a Shovel, do so and mark it on your *Action Chart* as a Backpack Item. Due to the size of these tools, they each take up the same amount of space as two normal Backpack Items.

Two tunnels lead away from the chamber. One heads west, the other south.

If you wish to take the west tunnel, turn to **54**.
If you wish to take the south tunnel, turn to **129**.

323

You release the arrow and it whistles through the air and buries itself deeply into the mail-clad shoulder of the bandit-leader. You hear his scream of pain ring out above the din of battle, but even though he is badly wounded he still attempts to rally his men. You stoop to take another arrow, but, to your horror, the dead soldier's quiver is empty. Looking up you see two dismounted Vassagonian horsemen clambering across the barricade towards you. You throw down your bow and run to a large water cask defended by a stout Sommlending sergeant. The ground around the cask is carpeted with enemy dead.

'Shoot the leader!' you command, pointing towards the enemy officer. The sergeant aims and fires his bow with one swift and fluid movement. The arrow arcs through the battle-smoke and pierces the officer's shiny breastplate. Slowly his cruel eyes flicker and close as he slips from the saddle, the shaft lodged deep in his heart.

Turn to **148**.

324

You are hungry and must eat a Meal before you sleep or lose 3 ENDURANCE points. You have been asleep for only two hours when you are awoken by the sound of a tolling bell.

'Bandits!' screams the tavern-keeper. 'They've got into the stables!'

You must act quickly or the bandits will steal your horses. The tavern-keeper tells you that there are two ways to the stables from here: you can either leave through the front door and run around to the side of the tavern, or climb the stairs to the first floor window and jump down on to the stable roof.

If you wish to use the front door, turn to **114**.
If you wish to jump from the first floor window, turn to **196**.

325

You are in combat with Barraka, renegade noble of Vassagonia. You cannot evade the combat and must fight to the death. He is a formidable warrior who possesses great strength of will and he is immune to Mindblast.

Barraka: COMBAT SKILL 25   ENDURANCE 29

If you win the combat, turn to **350**.

326

You suddenly realize that you have entered a remote section of the Maaken mines via a disused passage from the foothills of the Maaken range. For hundreds of years, the ore of this range has been the blessing and the bane of thousands drawn here to seek their fortune. Men have either found wealth beyond their wildest dreams, or have perished without trace in the labyrinth of cold, damp tunnels. You know that if only you can locate a section of this mine that is still in use, you will be able to follow its tunnels all the way to Ruanon itself. As Ruanon lies to the south you decide to take the south passage out of the chamber.

Turn to **101**.

327

You draw the sword and offer it to the Captain. A look of surprise and delight crosses his face as he examines the blade. 'I never expected to see my trusty steel again. It is a good omen for the battle ahead.'

Thanking you, the Captain sheathes his sword in its scabbard, that until now, has hung empty from his belt.

Turn to **289**.

328

As you reach the top of the ridge, a gruesome sight meets you. The bodies of men and horses lie scattered across the shallow valley beyond, their bones picked clean by the scavenging crows. You hear the gasps of horror as your men recognize the armour and tattered white uniforms of these skeletons, for they were once your countrymen, Sommlending Guards of the King's cavalry. They must have died in battle, for the corpses of bandit warriors lie entwined among them. Forty brave soldiers, nearly half of the squadron that left Holmgard one month ago, now lie

before you, and it is with heavy heart that your men set about the grisly task of burial. As you ride away from this valley of death, you are comforted only by the knowledge that Captain D'Val was not among those you buried.

Turn to **120**.

329

The river fills your ears, your eyes and your nose. In your desperate fight for air you cough uncontrollably. Blinded by water, you fail to see the large river boulder looming ahead. With a sickening crack, you smash head first into the unyielding stone and sink beneath the rushing torrent.

Your life and your mission end here.

330

At first light, you prepare to enter the valley. The highway is enshrouded by mist and soon, on both sides, the Ruanon forest closes in; a tangle of pale grey tree-trunks of every shape and size crowd thickly around you. After a few minutes ride, you find the wreck of a burnt-out wagon abandoned at the side of the road. Behind it, a track disappears eastwards into the hills.

If you wish to search the wrecked wagon, turn to **38**.

If you wish to ignore the wagon and press on along the highway, turn to **175**.

If you wish to investigate the track that leads up into the hills, turn to **293**.

331

You soon discover a partially concealed mine shaft descending vertically into the hillside. As your men clear away the briars choking the shaft, you notice a ladder fixed to one side. You realize that this must be an escape shaft from the Maaken mines, for they honeycomb the foothills of this mountain range. If only you can locate a major tunnel, you may find a path all the way to Ruanon itself. You kneel at the edge and peer down into the gloom. There is such an overwhelming smell of dampness and decay that you decide to send your lightest man down the ladder to check whether it is still secure. All seems well, for he soon reaches a tunnel entrance far below and shouts to you all to follow.

The tunnel leads to an oval-shaped, rough-hewn chamber, the floor of which is coated with a strange silky fluid.

If you have the Kai Discipline of Animal Kinship, turn to **41**.

If you do not have this skill, you can search for an exit from the chamber and turn to **276**.

332

Although the wagons are shrouded in darkness, your Kai sense reveals to you the actor's hiding place. You climb the ladder at the rear of a large caravan, push open the door with your weapon, and enter.

Turn to **222**.

333

The horseman is charging at you very quickly. You will only be able to fight for *one* round of combat before the momentum of his attack carries him past you.

Vassagonian Horseman:
COMBAT SKILL 20   ENDURANCE 28

If you lose more ENDURANCE points than your enemy in this one round of combat, turn to **209**.

If your enemy loses more ENDURANCE points than you in this round of combat, turn to **220**.

If you both lose exactly the same number of ENDURANCE points in this round of combat, turn to **344**.

334

As you hit the water, your weapon is jarred from your hand. Panic overwhelms your senses as slimy tentacles coil around your sinking body. You fight to escape but are soon squeezed into unconsciousness. A trail of bubbles and a torn cloak are the only signs to mark your watery grave.

Your life and your mission end here.

335

The tunnel soon emerges into a large chamber divided by a deep mine shaft. A dark-skinned warrior in tatty leather armour stands guard at the entrance to the wooden bridge spanning the shaft. He is whittling a block of wood and grumbling to himself about how unfair it is that he is given the most boring duties. On the far side of the chamber a tunnel disappears into the west wall. You know that if you are to reach the tunnel, you must get past the guard and across the bridge.

If you possess the Kai Discipline of Camouflage, turn to **35**.

If you have the Kai Discipline of Mind Over Matter, turn to **317**.

If you possess neither of the above Kai Disciplines, you will have to launch a surprise attack on the guard. Turn to **147**.

336

The arrow flies straight and true towards the bandit but glances off his polished steel breastplate. Unmoved by this close escape from death, he hurls his javelin, pinning the helpless soldier to the ground. You are about to take another shot when you see a menacing black shape dart across the sky; it plummets downwards and lands on the watchtower roof.

You discard your bow and draw your weapon as you race up the stairs to investigate.

Turn to **223**.

337

Although fire has totally destroyed any markings there may have been on the wagon, there still remains enough of the shell for you to recognise its military origin. It is a Sommlending cavalry wagon, one of three that accompanied Captain D'Val and his troopers. It was loaded with provisions when it left Holmgard a month ago, but now all that remains of its cargo are heaps of ash. Having made a thorough search of the wreckage, you remount your horse and lead your men southwards along the highway.

Turn to **297**.

338

Your bravado has paid off. The guards accept the password and allow you to enter the crypt. As the stone door is drawn shut, you find yourself in a wide torchlit corridor heading towards the east.

Turn to **235**.

339

Although the strangers seem harmless enough, you decide not to take any chances and mount a guard. You are hungry and must eat a Meal or lose 3 ENDURANCE points. Having eaten, you soon settle down to get a good night's sleep.

Turn to **233**.

340

Your head begins to spin and your legs feel as heavy as lead from the lack of oxygen. You lose 2 ENDURANCE points.

Turn to **32**.

341

A circle of unshaven faces are staring down at you. A soldier cradles your leg as another snaps the shaft

342

buried deeply in your thigh. But before you can even cry out in pain, he has drawn the arrow from your leg with one swift tug. 'You are very lucky, Kai Lord,' he says, as he bandages a handful of Laumspur to your aching limb. 'The wound is clean and the bleeding is but slight.'

You lose 4 ENDURANCE points, but the soldier's quick thinking and skill has saved your leg from infection. With great care the soldiers carry both you and Captain D'Val into the stone watchtower.

Turn to **116**.

342

You plummet head first into the darkness, the wind screaming past your face. Gritting your teeth you try not to think of that terrible moment of impact, when you will smash into the hard unyielding rock. But instead of a stone floor you hit the surface of an underground river and plunge far down into its icy cold depths. You are so relieved to be alive that you momentarily forget where you are and inhale. As water enters your lungs, you fight to control the pain that now wracks your chest. You quickly become aware that your Backpack is dragging you down. You must discard it or you will surely drown. When you eventually reach the surface, you claw your way out of the icy water and collapse on a gravel bank, coughing and gasping for air.

You have lost your Backpack and everything that it contained, but you are still alive and relatively unharmed. Make the necessary adjustments to your *Action Chart* before turning to **219**.

343 – *Illustration XX (overleaf)*

You are halfway across the underground river when the inky black water begins to seethe and boil. You cling to the gunwale and urge your men to row for all they are worth, for the turbulent water now threatens to capsize your crowded little boat. Suddenly a hideous greyish green tentacle breaks through the surface. Like a whiplash it crashes down, splintering wood and cracking bone as it coils around two of your men. Before you can even draw your weapon, they have been dragged down into the bubbling depths. Then another tentacle rises, snaking towards you. It stabs at your chest and tries to butt you overboard.

Pick a number from the *Random Number Table*. If your current ENDURANCE point total is 20 or more, add 3 to the number that you have picked. If your current ENDURANCE point total is 12 or less, deduct 2 from the number you have picked.

If your total is now −2–6, turn to **194**.
If it is 7–12, turn to **61**.

344

Your blow has splintered the horseman's lance. As he reins his horse about, he discards his broken weapon and draws a curved broadsword. His smile is evil, exposing a jagged line of blackened teeth. He spits a battle-cry and spurs his horse towards you once more.

If you have reached the Kai rank of Aspirant or higher, turn to **111**.
If you have not yet reached this level of Kai training, turn to **43**.

XX.   The Rangers are dragged down into the bubbling depths

345

You search the stalls to discover that only eleven horses remain; the others have been stolen by the bandits. After careful thought, you decide to call for ten volunteers to continue the mission with you, and order the remaining rangers to return to Sommerlund on foot at first light to report what has happened. As they head off to the north at dawn, you wait until they have vanished from sight before you turn and ride in the opposite direction.

Pick a number from the *Random Number Table*.

If the number you have picked is *0–6*, turn to **51**.
If it is *7–9*, turn to **120**.

346

For over five minutes you climb the spiral staircase before reaching the next level, where a mine tunnel leads off towards the south. You have covered less than a hundred yards of the dank passage when you discover a lever, set high up on the left hand wall. A sudden noise in the distance betrays a guard patrol marching towards you. Without a second thought you pull the lever and a stone panel slides back to reveal a secret tunnel. You enter quickly to avoid the guards. Once they have passed by, you try to leave but find that you cannot re-open the stone panel from the inside. With a growing feeling of despair, you turn and follow the secret tunnel.

Turn to **335**.

347

You are at the bottom of the cellar ladder when the trapdoor slams shut and you hear a drawbolt slide across and lock. You hammer on the trapdoor, desperately trying to escape but your captors cover the trapdoor with a heavy oak cask and keep guard in the room above. Four days pass before the lock slides back; but the hands that open the trapdoor are bony and fleshless.

Your life and your mission end here.

348

Less than fifty yards along the tunnel wall you notice a lever. Your Kai instincts make you naturally suspicious of this unusual feature, and you scour the floor looking for evidence of a trap. You find nothing, but a glance at the the roof reveals the underside of a wide portcullis hidden between two beams.

You pull the lever and the portcullis falls, sealing off the tunnel behind you. To make sure you will not be followed, you smash the lever with a wedge of stone before continuing along the tunnel.

Turn to **185**.

349

Judging by the smoothness of the stone floor and the condition of the ore wagons, you deduce that this gallery must service a major section of the mines. A fresh breeze can be felt blowing out of the west tunnel and you sense that you must be near the surface.

Ruanon lies due west, the same direction as the ore wagon tunnel. You take a deep breath and emerge from the shadows, cross the gallery, and quietly enter the archway beyond.

Turn to **55**.

As Barraka dies, the wind suddenly rises in pitch and intensity, filling the temple with a mournful cry of despair. You feel the chill, malevolent spirit of Dark-lord Vashna engulfing you in an icy embrace, but you sense that he is powerless to harm you. The sacrifice has been foiled; he is doomed to lament for a victory that might have been.

Lying on the black temple floor is the Dagger of Vashna. As you pick it up and tuck it into your belt (mark this on your *Action Chart* as a Special Item), the evil blue flame flickers and dies. As long as you possess this evil blade, Darklord Vashna and his legion of dead warriors will remain imprisoned in the chasm of doom.

You free fair Madelon from the altar and carry her through the corridors of the temple that lead up to the surface. As you emerge into the moonlit ruins, an astounding sight greets your eyes. Barraka's warriors are running from the ghost city in all directions, closely pursued by an army of cavalrymen. The light of the full moon and the guttering torches that these horsemen carry, illuminates the sun-crest that bedecks their tunics. Word must have reached Holmgard for they are the Sommlending army, led by King Ulnar himself. Your countrymen praise your courage and daring, their strident cheers drowning the cry of Maakengorge; for once again you have proved yourself a true hero of Sommerlund. As you deliver Madelon into the waiting arms of her father, his overwhelming joy fills you with a sense of great achievement. You are indeed worthy of the title 'Kai Lord'. You have succeeded in your perilous quest,

XXI.   Barraka's men flee from King Ulnar and the army of
Sommerlund

but the epic saga of Lone Wolf – last of the Kai Lords – is far from complete. A new and deadly challenge awaits you in Book 5 of the Lone Wolf series entitled:

Shadow on the Sand

* * *

THE LONE WOLF CLUB

The Lone Wolf Club offers you exciting opportunities to become further involved in Lone Wolf activities. Joe Dever and Gary Chalk will be writing a newsletter for the Club and there will be competitions, events and the opportunity to collect Lone Wolf souvenirs.

If you are interested in becoming a member of the Lone Wolf Club, please write to The Lone Wolf Club, Sparrow Books, 17–21 Conway Street, London W1P 6JD, enclosing a <u>large</u> stamped addressed envelope or an international money order to cover postage if you live abroad or in Ireland.

CITADEL MINIATURES

A unique range of Lone Wolf models, especially designed by Gary Chalk and Joe Dever, are now available from Citadel miniatures from around 40p. For details of these and Citadel's extensive range of over 1000 models, please send a stamped addressed envelope to Citadel Miniatures, Chewton Street, Hilltop, Eastwood, Notts.

Citadel miniatures are made especially for gamers and collectors. They are lead models and therefore not for use by young children.

LONE WOLF SOFTWARE

Fully interactive software adventure games for Lone Wolf 1 & 2 are available for owners of the Sinclair ZX Spectrum 48K. A special feature of the program is a training sequence at the start of the game, in which the player fights with one of his teachers to set his COMBAT SKILLS for the Lone Wolf adventures.

Lone Wolf software will be available in bookshops and computer stores as a book-plus-cassette package. The cassette-only version can be ordered directly from the publishers at £6.95 each (includes VAT, postage and packing).

Send your order and cheque/postal order, made payable to the Hutchinson Publishing Group, to: Hutchinson Computer Publishing Ltd, 17–21 Conway Street, London W1P 6JD.

State clearly which program you require and allow 14 days for delivery.

RANDOM NUMBER TABLE

1	3	9	3	2	7	5	0	2	5
5	6	2	5	1	3	8	4	3	5
7	6	7	8	1	4	3	1	4	5
4	0	8	7	3	0	8	7	2	5
7	4	0	0	9	6	2	0	8	1
1	6	7	9	6	9	0	3	3	9
8	9	2	8	1	3	4	9	7	1
6	3	0	7	5	0	5	4	6	6
7	2	1	4	2	9	6	4	2	6
0	9	6	4	8	2	8	5	8	3